Contents

Acknowledgments

....

Mille mercis to my French friends who are
responsible for many of the recipes in this book;
in particular to Georgette Oddon, Juliette Rasclard,
Paule Basiaux, Lorette Noudel, Jeanine Nouailles,
and Maurice Pinard.

A thousand thanks to my American students and
friends who helped to test the recipes here in New York
and in Arizona. Thank you, Amanda Berman,
Christina Dieckman, Patti Hart, Nan Chisholm,
Nancy Moran, and Betti Zucker.

I cannot forget to thank my husband, Wayne,
my best critic, and my editor, Susan Friedland, who
used her "magic" to make this book enjoyable.

Introduction

....

WHEN YOU FOLLOW the river Drôme to its source, you arrive in the small village of Valdrôme (population less than one hundred, and getting smaller every year), and you continue driving for two miles to Brézès on a one-lane dirt road to the end of a small canyon—that's where my grandfather lived.

For twenty summers, until the summer of 1989, my husband and I lived in my grandfather's house. We were accepted by the locals because I was Joel Aubert's granddaughter. My experiences there could be out of the pages of Marcel Pagnol's stories of *Jean de Florette* and *Manon des Sources*.

Pagnol portrays the greed and envy of peasants when water is a problem. Water means survival in Provence. If you own a spring that does not dry up during the summer months, you are safe from a catastrophe. My grandfather had such a spring, but it was not near his house. Three families lived in Brézès: the Auberts (my grandfather), the Oddons (the good neighbors), and the Chaberts (the bad neighbors). The most direct route to my grandfather's spring was a fifteen-minute walk, but he would have had to cross Chabert's field, which was unthinkable. Every few days he harnessed his mule, Bijoune, straddling the animal with water bottles for the one-hour trek to his spring high on the side of Tarsimour, the hill that ends the canyon. He walked back home while Bijoune carried the load. He followed this routine until the day he died in 1935.

But for us in 1966, running water was essential. I could not see us on a mule looking for water. Ernest Oddon, our good neighbor, and my husband, Wayne, talked endlessly on how to tap into our spring, which never dries up; unfortunately, it meant blasting away most of the side of Tarsimour.

"Well," said Wayne, master of the easy way out, "we have a small creek in front of the house. Why not tap that water?"

"No," said Ernest.

"But why not?"

"It's polluted."

"But, Ernest, how can it be polluted? We are at the end of a canyon road, the creek comes from Tarsimour. Is there anyone living on top of Tarsimour?"

"No."

"Then why not drink it?"

"Well," said Ernest, "there are foxes up there; and I'm sure they pee in the creek."

That was that and Ernest was right. Subsequently I read about foxes contaminating water in creeks. We finally chose a spring owned by Ernest, but we had to let the bad neighbor in because the conduit had to pass through his field. Today Brézès has running water but once in a while when the bad neighbor is bad, he'll sneak out in the middle of the night to pull out the plugs of the water reservoir and then we have no water for two days.

After spending so many peaceful summers there, in the hills of a forgotten land, we moved fifty miles southwest, back to civilization into the remains of a medieval château in Nyons, a small town where the western Provençal plains begin. And we made the move all because of vinegar!

That fateful spring of 1989, my husband decided to produce vinegar on a grand scale; Wayne is very proud of his vinegar and up until then had made it in a thirty-gallon wine keg in our New York house. It seems that suddenly the urge to create more hassles in our lives became imperative. Clark Wolf, a consultant for gourmet stores and restaurants, generously advised Wayne that indeed it was possible and could be lucrative to make and import vinegar from France. I admit that I was taken more with the idea of looking for real estate, my real passion in life, than making vinegar in France.

Wayne wanted a barn in Carpentras (a town at the foot of Mont Ventoux), but I wanted a house in Nyons. I had been coming down from the hills every Thursday morning for the last ten summers to shop at the weekly local market of Nyons, the olive capital. I had a soft spot in my heart for Nyons; my mother and aunt were born near there, in a village surrounded by olive groves. Driving down through the gorge of St. May to Nyons I learned to spot the most northern olive trees in France. It's a beautiful rural and sunny place where olive, apricot, and cherry orchards grace the hills; it's also in the heart of the Côtes du Rhône wines, from Châteauneuf du Pape to Gigondas to Vinsobres vineyards, ideal places to find a barn for Wayne's vinegar.

We started looking at a huge dilapidated barn, but quickly the search was on for a house and a barn. On August 24, 1989, we both fell in love with the château in Nyons. It ended the vinegar story because the armory, the only place suitable for making it, is too cold. With our purchase, I started cooking classes in the château and continued my long love affair with the Midi.

My French Kitchen

I LOVE MY KITCHEN in Nyons even though it has only a bare minimum of modern conveniences. The former owner of the château was an artist, not a cook. She hid the sink in an armoire and the stove in a credenza! Every time you wanted to use the sink you had to open doors and (invariably) you bumped your head on the front of the armoire. Armoire and credenza had to go; otherwise, we left the kitchen very much as it was. It's an old-fashioned kitchen, on two levels, with an ancient flagstone floor, furnished with antiques, adorned with shiny copper pots and Provençal pottery from Cliousclat and Dieulefit, the northern Provençal pottery center. It gets high marks for charm, but it's low on convenience. There are no proper counters to prepare a meal, only tables. If you are short, like me, it's no problem to cut and chop, but if you are tall, your back breaks. Perhaps one day I'll renovate to put in what the French contractors call *une cuisine américaine* (fitted cupboards and counters flush with kitchen appliances), but I know a lot of its personality will be sacrificed.

I fantasize that my kitchen was also the kitchen of the château in the Middle Ages. Kitchens and sculleries never had the best orientation in the planning of rooms, and mine is dark, facing northwest. But it's a delight in the summer—the western sun hits it toward the end of the afternoon, just when I am ready to cook. The sun is not too hot then and it makes me and the room very cheerful. I am ready for my favorite activity, cooking.

During the summer I entertain all the time, so much so that when October comes, I am ready to go back to New York, where I entertain on a much smaller scale. "If you own a house in the Midi," my French friends say, "you are everybody's friend. It's the region of France where the sun shines the most."

My meals are not elaborate; they are simple and seasonal meals. Typically, we start with a glass of wine and the olives of Nyons. I follow with a barbecued meat, a vegetable, and a green salad; for dessert, we have fruit or a fruit tart. For special occasions, I make either a more elaborate first course or a main course that involves more cooking than just barbecuing.

I love to cook but I refuse to spend hours in the kitchen, where I tire and am isolated from my guests. Since my friends tend to stay with us for at least a week, every one has to participate in meal preparation. I don't mind teaching them as long as I don't have to prep and clean dishes! It works out very well, and it gives me an opportunity to test recipes.

I cook in Nyons from mid-May to the end of September, the months when herbs abound. In the hills, back of Nyons and in Brézès, I send my husband to pick bundles of wild thyme. (Unfortunately, I am unable to stand the heavenly but very pungent scent of large patches of wild thyme; my head spins and I faint!) We dry the thyme in small bouquets, hanging them upside down on rafters in the armory of the château or in the barn at Brézès.

A rosemary bush taller than me gives shade to the garden; I make large bouquets of roses and rosemary branches to decorate my kitchen besides flavoring dishes with the fragrant herb.

Sage covers half the ground of my small garden; I use it sparingly in cooking, but again I make great bouquets, combining it with lavender in July when the lavender blooms. I also dry small bouquets of sage next to the thyme.

I cultivate basil and sorrel, which I use only during the summer in salad greens.

I dry orange peels on a fine-mesh stretcher (I dry lavender the same way) in a well-ventilated room (in Brézès, it's a barn, in Nyons, it's the armory of the château). I put them in daubes and bouillabaisses.

Salted anchovies and Nyons olives are always present in my pantry. I keep olives in brine in an old crockery pot that belonged to my grandfather.

To cure your own olives as they do in the Midi, make a brine of salt and water in a ratio of 1 to 10; add the olives, cover, and reserve in a cool place for about 4 months. Store them in the brine and remove the olives with a slotted spoon or a perforated olive wood scoop.

When I am in New York, I substitute anchovy fillets in oil for the salt and I use Niçoise or Gaeta olives.

In my kitchen, the two basic ingredients placed on the table next to the stove are Nyons olive oil and my husband Wayne's vinegar.

On Olive Oil

DURING THE CHRISTMAS holidays, I take my two 10-liter glass demijohns (large bottles now found at flea markets for lamp bases) to my favorite olive mill down by the river Eygues, where I have them filled with olive oil, the liquid gold of Nyons.

Olive oil from Nyons is the only one in France that boasts an *appéllation d'origine.* It is made exclusively with olives from Nyons, a variety called La Tanche. The olives ripen on the trees and are picked in December. Many Nyonsais harvest olives from their trees, then go to one of the three olive mills in town to have their year's supply of olive oil made.

First the olives are sorted; large and medium olives are sold to markets and small olives are kept for making oil. They are thrown into large vats and crushed to a paste by stone rollers. In Nyons, the millers still use the ancient Greek technique of crushing olives together with the pits. The pit has an almond that keeps the oil fresh for over a year without need for a chemical preservative.

The olive paste is spread on round nylon fiber mats called *scourtins;* old-fashioned coco fiber *scourtins* are still made to decorate bathroom and kitchen floors. The mats loaded with olive paste are stacked, a hundred at a time, on a compressor and pressed down to extract a black syrupy liquid, a mixture of water and oil. The oil and water are then separated in a centrifuge; the water, black from the non-oily part of the olive, is discarded while the oil is filtered through cotton, becoming liquid gold. Olive oil purists do not filter; according to them, sediment gives the oil more character. To filter or not to filter is a raging battle too in the wine industry.

And like wine, the character of an olive oil depends on the soil, the orientation of the land, the variety of olives, as well as on the method of making it. I mentioned the traditional method above, but large cooperatives, Nyons included, have more sophisticated machines to extract oil.

Quality olive oil is always made from the first cold pressing of the olives. Extra-virgin and virgin olive oil are labels that indicate a first cold pressing. Which olive oil is the best? It's a matter of taste. I am partial to the oil in Nyons for obvious reasons; I am proud to live there and I favor the mild flavor of its olive oil made from ripe olives; on the other hand, most of my students prefer a more robust olive oil made from a mixture of olives, including unripe ones.

For cooking, I recommend a mild-tasting olive oil because fragrant oils will overpower the dish. When I make aioli (garlic mayonnaise), I cut the olive oil with corn oil.

In Nyons, in years past, the olive pulp after the first pressing was made into compost to be spread on the stumps of the olive trees or was sold to make soap. Today, it is sold to greenhouses for fuel.

On the first Sunday of February, Nyons readies itself for L'Alicoque, the feast celebrating and blessing the brand-new oil of the year. There's a parade of the knights of olive oil, all decked out in their olive green velvety costumes and their Robin Hood hats adorned with a branch of olive tree. Last year, 12,000 croutons rubbed with garlic and oil were eaten in less than two hours (a lot for a small town); all this, of course, washed down with wines of the region.

Wayne's Vinegar

ONE DAY, MY husband chose a bottle of red wine that had been sitting in the basement for quite a while. When he saw the neck of the bottle was broken, he started to pour the wine into the sink but quickly stopped when he realized that it had turned into fragrant vinegar. I haven't bought wine vinegar since then! Once his vinegar won a vinegar tasting, against such competition. His secret is simplicity. Today, we have a large wine barrel that makes about 20 gallons of vinegar a year, barely enough for friends and family.

Whenever we don't finish a bottle of wine, we gather all the leftovers and when we have enough for a half-gallon bottle, we pour in 1 cup of excellent commercial wine vinegar, cover the top with muslin, and then leave the jug for 3 months or more. The wine should be relatively free of chemicals, otherwise the alcohol in the wine will not turn into acetic acid to make vinegar, and the bottle, jug, or barrel should be kept in a warm place (75 to 80 degrees), such as next to a fireplace or radiator.

THE OLIVE OIL and Wayne's vinegar are the two indispensable staples in my kitchen; other prepared foods I have always in hand keep in the refrigerator for several weeks, or, in the case of the broth, freeze well. Cooking is much simpler when I can reach for a tomato sauce or a broth to prepare a dish.

Marmelade de poivrons rouges

Red Pepper Marmalade

DURING THE SUMMER, I keep bowls of red peppers marinating in olive oil and garlic in my refrigerator. I eat them in sandwiches, over pasta, or as a salad course.

MAKES 4 CUPS

6 large red bell peppers	2 large garlic cloves, minced
1½ teaspoons salt	2 tablespoons olive oil

Preheat the oven to 450 degrees.

Line a broiler pan with aluminum foil and roast the peppers in the upper part of the oven for 20 to 30 minutes, turning over occasionally until soft. (You may also barbecue the peppers on hot coals.)

Place the peppers in a heavy plastic bag and set aside until cool.

Peel the peppers. Quarter them over a plate to catch the juice that spews out. Discard the core and seeds.

In a mixing bowl, combine the peppers, juice, salt, garlic, and olive oil. Cover and refrigerate until needed. The marmalade will keep for 2 to 3 weeks. Return to room temperature before serving.

Around the Making of a Tomato Sauce

YEARS AGO, I canned batches and batches of tomato sauce in my New York kitchen without peeling and seeding the tomatoes. I strained the amount of sauce I needed as I needed it. In my French kitchen for the last five years, I've changed techniques: I peel and seed the tomatoes before making the sauce, just as my friends do here in the Midi. Susan Friedland, my editor and friend, was in Nyons visiting and working with me on this book. She hates peeling tomatoes and we got into a friendly argument on which is more work: peeling and seeding the tomatoes before making the sauce or straining the cooked sauce to discard the peel and seeds.

To resolve this important question of peeling, I mobilized my numerous houseguests on that particular day to test the different methods. We made one batch with peeled and seeded tomatoes; another with unpeeled, unseeded tomatoes. We strained half the unpeeled batch.

As I suspected, we ended up liking all three tomato sauces, with a slight preference for the strained one. The unstrained sauce was very good, though it had a rougher texture than the others. The tomato sauce made with peeled and seeded tomatoes was fine notwithstanding one of the guests' complaints about finding a seed in it!

I find peeling and seeding tomatoes no more work than straining tomato sauce; Susan thinks straining takes less time. Fortunately, we did not test the sauce again to clock the peeling-seeding technique against the straining technique! We already had enough tomato sauce!

I give instructions for the three methods and you decide.

Coulis de tomates d'été

Summer Tomato Sauce

MAKES 5 CUPS OF THICK SAUCE

5 tablespoons olive oil

1½ cups sliced onions

5 large garlic cloves, coarsely
chopped

5 pounds large tomatoes,
chopped (15 cups), or
peeled, seeded, and
chopped (10 cups)
(see Note)

1½ teaspoons sugar

2 teaspoons salt

Freshly ground black pepper

½ cup basil leaves

In a large saucepan, heat the oil over medium heat. Cook the onions and garlic without burning, for 5 minutes, stirring occasionally.

Stir in the tomatoes, sugar, salt, pepper, and basil. Cook over high heat, stirring occasionally, for 30 to 35 minutes for the unpeeled version or 20 to 25 minutes for the peeled tomatoes (the timing depends largely on the juiciness of the tomatoes). The consistency should be like that of a very soft relish.

In a food processor, puree the tomatoes in 2 batches for 1 minute each. In all, the sauce yields about 5 cups; if there is more, boil it down to concentrate if you wish.

Taste and correct seasoning.

For the tomato sauce made with unpeeled tomatoes, eat as is or strain. You can do a test to see if it's worth the work. To strain the sauce, pour half into a large meshed kitchen strainer placed over a large bowl. With the back of a large spoon or with a wooden spatula, push down to extract all the sauce. Discard the skins and seeds (this takes about 5 minutes).

For the sauce made with peeled and seeded tomatoes, set aside to cool before refrigerating.

The sauce lasts 3 to 4 weeks in the refrigerator. I serve it over pasta and use it for several recipes such as Veal Breast Spareribs with Fresh Tomatoes (page 160) or Rabbit with Fresh Savory in a Tomato Sauce (page 137).

NOTE:

To peel tomatoes, bring several quarts of water to a boil. Drop 4 to 5 tomatoes in the boiling water for 15 seconds for ripe tomatoes, 30 seconds for firmer tomatoes. With a slotted spoon, transfer them to a bowl of cold water for 30 seconds or so. The skins should easily slip off the tomatoes.

To Can Tomato Sauce

Sterilize jars by submerging them in boiling water.

Sterilize tongs, lids, rings, ladle, and funnel in boiling water for 5 minutes.

Try to keep the jars and the tomato sauce hot during the canning process.

Fit a canning funnel in the mouth of the jar and fill up to ½ inch of the top. Wipe the rim with a clean towel.

Using tongs, remove a lid from the hot water and place it on the filled jar. Then screw the ring on tightly.

Place the jars in the rack of the water bath canner and gently lower the rack into boiling water. Make sure the jars are covered by at least 1 inch of water. Cover the canner and boil the jars 35 minutes for quarts and 25 minutes for pints.

Remove the rack from the canner and set aside to cool.

If the jar spontaneously gives a "plinking" or "pinging" sound while cooling, the jar is sealed. When the jars are cold, push the center of the lid down with your index finger; if it does not spring back, the jar is sealed. If the lid springs back, reprocess the jar.

Coulis de tomates avec des tomates en boîte

Tomato Sauce Made with Canned Tomatoes

CANNED TOMATOES MAKE good tomato sauce. I buy whole peeled Italian-style tomatoes. I avoid crushed tomatoes and tomatoes packed in tomato puree. This is a thick sauce.

MAKES 6 CUPS

⅓ cup olive oil

2 onions, thinly sliced (2 cups)

3 large garlic cloves, minced

Three 28-ounce cans Italian plum tomatoes, drained (reserve juice) and chopped

2 teaspoons sugar

2 teaspoons salt

Freshly ground black pepper

⅓ cup minced parsley

In a very large skillet or 2 medium skillets, heat the olive oil over medium heat. Cook the onions and garlic for 5 minutes without burning, occasionally stirring.

Add the tomatoes, sugar, salt, pepper, and parsley. Cook over high heat for 25 minutes, ladling in all the reserved tomato juice every so often; reduce before adding another ladleful.

In a food processor, puree the tomatoes in batches for 1 minute or until smooth. Taste and adjust seasoning.

VARIATION

Spicy Tomato Sauce

Add a little less than ⅛ teaspoon ground cayenne with the sugar and salt to this sauce and to the one made from fresh tomatoes (page 8).

Bouillon léger

Light Broth

IF YOU REALLY want to make homemade broth (and there is nothing better), get to know a butcher and he will keep you supplied with chicken, beef, or veal bones for your next big batch of broth. Every week, I make chicken broth for soups. Dominic Gaimaro and Robert Tramontana, my butchers in New York, and Guy Dinelle in Nyons keep chicken scraps (necks, carcasses, etc.) for me and sometimes they add a veal or beef bone.

MAKES 3 QUARTS

5 pounds chicken necks or carcasses and/or veal or beef bones

1 pound carrots, unpeeled, coarsely chopped

2 celery branches, coarsely chopped

1 large unpeeled onion, stuck with 4 cloves and quartered

Several sprigs of fresh thyme or 2 teaspoons dry thyme wrapped in cheesecloth

A bouquet of Italian parsley

2 tablespoons salt

In a large stockpot, cover the bones with 6 quarts of water. Bring the water to a boil and skim the scum from the surface.

Add all the vegetables, herbs, and salt. Cover partially and reduce over medium heat to 3 quarts of broth (about 3 to 4 hours), occasionally discarding the fat that rises to the surface.

Strain the broth. Pick out any meat on the bones and reserve for sandwiches, soups, or salads. Set the broth aside to cool and refrigerate or freeze. Boil the broth every 4 to 5 days if it is refrigerated; it can keep undisturbed if frozen.

Bouillon concentré

1-Hour Rich Broth

THIS IS A painless way to make a rich broth quickly. I reserve the cooked meat and vegetables for a family dinner or for sandwiches. I serve it with aioli (garlic mayonnaise) or horseradish. It's important to use meat with bones instead of just bones for the broth. It needs to cook very fast and the meat will release flavor faster than bones alone.

When I need more than 3 cups of rich broth, I make 2 batches; that works out better than doubling the recipe.

MAKES 3 CUPS

3 tablespoons olive oil

1½ pounds veal breast, fat trimmed and cut into pieces, stewing beef, or chicken parts

1 cup ½-inch slices celeriac (celery root)

1 cup ½-inch slices washed leek (white and green)

1 cup chopped onion

1 cup ½-inch slices carrots

1 cup ½-inch slices celery branch

1 cup chopped fresh tomatoes

Several sprigs of Italian parsley

2 teaspoons salt

In a very large skillet, heat the oil over medium high heat and brown the meat for 15 minutes.

Stir in the vegetables and brown for another 10 minutes. By this time, the kitchen should smell delicious.

Cover the meat, vegetables, and parsley with 5 cups water, or enough to cover.

Add salt and bring to a boil.

Cook down over medium to high heat to 3 cups, about 45 minutes, occasionally discarding fat that rises to top.

Strain the liquid and refrigerate.

Discard the fat on top of the rich broth.

Citrons confits

Preserved Lemons

I KEEP PRESERVED lemons in my refrigerator for several months. If you don't want to bother making them, buy them from specialty stores. I like looking at them in my refrigerator—they are very attractive in a glass jar.

If you live in California or Arizona and have lemon trees in your yard, you should make your own preserved lemons.

The lemony-salty flavor marries well with Chicken Fricassee (page 126) or Sweetbreads with Rosemary (page 167).

4 lemons, scrubbed under water   **1 cup white vinegar**

2 cups kosher salt

Cut each lemon lengthwise into 6 wedges, keeping them attached at the stem end.

In a bowl, combine the salt, vinegar, and 1 cup water.

Pack the lemons into a glass jar and pour the brine mixture over them. Cover and refrigerate for at least 2 weeks and up to 3 months.

To use, soak the lemons in cold water for several hours, occasionally changing water. Drain and proceed with the recipe.

Appetizers

Oignons à la grecque • 17
    (Pearl Onion Relish)

Caviar d'aubergines • 18
    (Eggplant Caviar)

Tapenade • 19

Tian d'aubergines et de tomates Vieux Télégraphe • 20
    (Cold Eggplant and Tomato Gratin Châteauneuf-du-Pape)

Le Risto • 21
    (Eggplant and Tomato from Arles)

Tomates farcies à la tomme et au basilic • 22
    (Stuffed Tomatoes with Ricotta and Basil)

Flan de courgettes au coulis de tomates fraîches • 23
    (Zucchini Flan with Tomato Sauce)

Terrine de jambon aux courgettes • 25
    (Ham and Zucchini Terrine)

La Bavaroise aux poivrons rouges • 26
    (Red Pepper Aspic)

Melon glacé au fromage blanc • 28
    (Cold Honeydew with Fresh Cheese)

I N S U M M E R I serve Nyons olives as an appetizer; in winter I serve slices of fresh and smoked mozzarella with baguettes. When I serve an appetizer for a special meal, I make sure to prepare a dish that can be made ahead. It gives me more time to spend on the courses that follow without getting tired.

All the recipes in this chapter are easily made a day ahead of time.

Oignons à la grecque

Pearl Onion Relish

I MAKE BATCHES of onion relish for Thanksgiving and Christmas holidays and I serve it along with rabbit pâté. The onions can be kept for several weeks in the refrigerator.

MAKES 1 QUART

$1\frac{1}{2}$ pounds pearl onions (see Note)

2 tablespoons olive oil

2 pounds fresh tomatoes, peeled, seeded, and chopped (4 cups) (see Note, page 9) or, in winter, one 28-ounce can Italian plum tomatoes, drained and chopped

$\frac{1}{2}$ cup shredded basil leaves

3 garlic cloves, minced

1 teaspoon salt

Freshly ground black pepper

1 cup golden raisins

1 tablespoon sugar

$\frac{1}{2}$ cup cider vinegar

$\frac{1}{2}$ cup Chardonnay

Plunge the onions into 2 quarts of boiling water for 1 minute. Drain and rinse under cold water. Peel the onions.

In a 6-quart dutch oven, heat the olive oil over medium high heat. Add the tomatoes, basil, garlic, salt, and pepper. Cook for 10 minutes partially covered, stirring occasionally.

Add the onions, raisins, sugar, vinegar, and wine. Cover and cook for 40 minutes over medium heat, stirring occasionally.

Taste and correct seasoning. Set aside to cool and refrigerate.

I keep the onions refrigerated for at least 6 weeks. I serve them with Shredded Rabbit Pâté (page 29) or as a condiment to go with roasts.

NOTE:

If pearl onions are unavailable, substitute canned pearl onions but not frozen; blanching is then unnecessary.

Caviar d'aubergines

Eggplant Caviar

I ALWAYS TAKE eggplant caviar on picnics to spread on crusty bread or for dipping cold chicken.

I make eggplant caviar a day ahead to let the flavors intensify. I keep it refrigerated for 2 weeks; it ages well.

MAKES 2 CUPS

½ pound fresh tomatoes, peeled, seeded, and chopped (½ cup) (see Note, page 9)

¾ teaspoon salt

1½ pounds eggplants

4 tablespoons plus 1 teaspoon olive oil

⅔ cup minced onion

4 garlic cloves, minced

4 teaspoons red wine vinegar

Freshly ground black pepper

Preheat the oven to 425 degrees.

In a strainer above a mixing bowl, sprinkle the tomatoes with ¼ teaspoon salt; let drain for 20 minutes.

Split each eggplant in half lengthwise. Drizzle 1 teaspoon oil over the cut tops. Place in a baking dish with ½ cup water and bake for 45 minutes or until tender. Turn them over after 20 minutes, adding more water if necessary. Set aside to cool.

With a teaspoon, scoop out the flesh of the eggplants.

In a food processor, puree the eggplant, the drained tomatoes, onion, garlic, remaining oil, vinegar, ½ teaspoon salt, and pepper for 1 minute.

Taste and correct seasoning.

Tapenade

TAPENADE IS A mixture of black olives, capers (*tapeno* in Provençal), and anchovies ground in a mortar. A blender or food processor works just as well as a mortar as long as the mixture is strained afterward to give it a creamy texture. I recommend that you taste the tapenade before and after passing it through a strainer.

Belton, who came along with his wife and friends to cook and live with me at the château the first summer I gave cooking lessons, asked for a tapenade. We decided to do a comparative study with a commercial version from Nyons and our own. Our tapenade had much more flavor than the commercial sample; so much so that Belton forgot the work it was to strain it. Fortunately a tapenade is used sparingly; half a teaspoon is plenty to spread on a toast.

Salt-packed anchovies are difficult to find in the States and even if you find them in ethnic food stores, half the time they are old and dried out; substitute anchovies in oil.

MAKES ½ CUP

1 scant cup pitted Niçoise or Gaeta olives

8 anchovy fillets in oil, patted dry

2 teaspoons drained capers

1 teaspoon Marc de Provence or grappa

42 Toasts (page 79)

In a food processor, process the olives, anchovies, capers, and brandy until very fine, occasionally scraping the work bowl.

Using the back of a spoon, force the mixture, 1 tablespoon at a time, through a strainer. Discard the skins that remain in the strainer before continuing with the next tablespoon.

This is a lot of work and the first time you do it, you'll wonder if the result is worth the effort. Have faith! It takes about 10 minutes to strain the whole amount and the results are delicious.

Spread ½ teaspoon tapenade on a toast. Tapenade refrigerates for 2 to 3 weeks.

Tian d'aubergines et de tomates Vieux Télégraphe

Cold Eggplant and Tomato Gratin Châteauneuf-du-Pape

MAGGIE BRUNIER, THE lovely hostess and owner of Le Vieux Télégraphe, a famous vineyard of Châteauneuf-du-Pape, is an excellent Provençal cook. During the summer, many visitors come to the winery to sample and buy wine; if you are lucky enough to be invited to one of her superb dinners, she might serve this cold platter of eggplant and tomatoes along with prosciutto, olives, and *Oignons à la grecque* (page 17). Her husband confided that he loves this dish but his favorite is still *Le Risto,* an Arlesian dish of eggplant and tomato sauce (opposite).

SERVES 10

2½ pounds eggplants, cut into ⅛- to 1/16-inch-thick slices (about 10 cups)

⅓ cup minced fresh thyme leaves and rosemary needles or 1 tablespoon dry herbs (thyme, rosemary, and oregano)

1 tablespoon salt

½ cup olive oil

3½ pounds firm fresh tomatoes, cut into ⅛- to 1/16-inch-thick slices (about 8 cups)

Preheat the oven to 400 degrees. Oil a 15 by 2-inch broiler pan.

In a large mixing bowl, toss the eggplant slices with the herbs, 1 teaspoon salt, and ⅓ cup oil.

In the prepared pan, make overlapping rows of eggplant and tomato slices. Fit them in as tightly as possible to fill the pan.

Dribble the remaining oil over the vegetables and sprinkle with the remaining salt.

Bake for 45 minutes; occasionally push gently on the vegetables with the back of a spoon.

Cover with foil and bake for another 30 minutes.

Set aside to cool. Serve at room temperature.

L e Risto

Eggplant and Tomato from Arles

TRADITIONALLY, THE *RISTO*, an old Provençal expression for this cold appetizer of eggplants, is served in a round black cast-iron pan, very much like a paella pan. In New York, I serve it in a black cast-iron skillet. If you prefer not to fry eggplants, see the recipe for Eggplant Gratin from the Vaucluse on page 200, in which the eggplants are boiled.

SERVES 6

2 cups corn oil

2 pounds eggplants, cut length-
    wise into ¼-inch-thick slices
    (about 8 cups)

Flour to dredge the eggplant

½ teaspoon salt

3 cups Summer Tomato Sauce
    (page 8)

In a large skillet, heat the oil to 325 degrees. Dredge the eggplant slices in flour just before frying them (do not dredge all the slices at once, they will become gummy while waiting to be fried); shake off excess.

Fry the eggplant slices carefully in several batches, turning occasionally. When they are a light golden color and cooked through, drain on several layers of paper towels.

Place a layer of eggplant slices in the bottom of a 10-inch round serving pan or in a black cast-iron skillet, sprinkle with salt, and dribble half the tomato sauce over the eggplant. Repeat with the remaining layer of eggplant and top with the rest of the tomato sauce.

Serve as is.

Tomates farcies à la tomme et au basilic

Stuffed Tomatoes with Ricotta and Basil

ONE THURSDAY, at the market in Nyons, I was contemplating a tomato stand, minding my own business, when the vendor suddenly told me that the night before she had stuffed tomatoes with goat cheese and basil with great success. It sounded like a winner: I quickly bought her tomatoes and basil, bought goat cheese, and rushed back home to cook stuffed tomatoes. It was a treat; I serve them nested in fresh pasta or on top of salad leaves.

In New York, I substitute fresh ricotta for the fresh goat cheese.

For best results, choose small tomatoes; the ratio of stuffing to tomato is important: a large tomato requires too much stuffing.

The stuffing on its own can be served as a dip with raw cauliflower, carrots, or broccoli.

SERVES 10

Ten 2–ounce tomatoes or large cherry tomatoes

1½ teaspoons salt

1 cup fresh ricotta cheese

¼ cup drained plain yogurt

2 large garlic cloves, coarsely chopped

1 cup basil leaves

1 tablespoon olive oil

Cut a ½-inch-thick slice from each tomato, opposite the stem end. Reserve the tomato "hats." Scoop out the pulp with a grapefruit spoon and reserve for a tomato sauce. Sprinkle ½ teaspoon salt among the tomato shells and drain upside down for 30 minutes.

In the bowl of a food processor, process the cheese, yogurt, garlic, basil, and remaining salt until smooth. Overfill each tomato and top each tomato with its hat. Place the tomatoes in a baking dish large enough to hold them barely touching. Dribble the olive oil over them. (Can be prepared to this point up to a day ahead of time.)

Preheat the oven to 400 degrees.

Bake the tomatoes for 15 to 20 minutes. Serve hot or warm.

By MIDSUMMER, ZUCCHINI and eggplants are taking over the kitchens of many amateur gardeners, all at their wits' end trying to think of one more way to cook those summer "invaders."

I don't cultivate these vegetables myself because somebody has to be their welcome recipient. As a thank you, I share with the growers these two recipes I created.

Flan de courgettes au coulis de tomates fraîches

Zucchini Flan with Tomato Sauce

To UNMOLD THE flan successfully, the zucchini puree needs to be well drained, otherwise, the flan will collapse.

SERVES 8 TO 10

4 pounds zucchini, peeled and cut into ½-inch cubes (12 cups)

½ cup basil leaves

4 eggs

¼ cup grated Gruyère cheese

1½ teaspoons salt

1 cup homemade bread crumbs

2 cups Summer Tomato Sauce (page 8)

¼ cup Niçoise or Gaeta olives

Preheat the oven to 400 degrees. Oil a 6-cup loaf pan (see Note).

Bring several quarts of salted water to a boil. Add the zucchini, and when the water returns to a boil cook the zucchini for 20 minutes or until tender. Drain.

In the food processor, puree the zucchini in batches until smooth. Let stand for 15 minutes in a fine-meshed kitchen strainer.

In the bowl of a food processor, process the drained zucchini puree with the basil, eggs, cheese, and salt until smooth.

With a spatula, fold in the bread crumbs. Taste and correct seasoning.

Pour the zucchini mixture into the prepared pan. Place the pan in a water bath that comes ⅔ of the way up the mold.

Bake in the center of the oven for 1 hour. Remove the pan from the water bath and set aside until cool.

continued

Run the blade of a knife around the sides of the pan. Unmold onto a serving platter, blot up any liquid that still might ooze out.

Serve at room temperature with the cold Summer Tomato Sauce and olives.

NOTE:

You can serve the flan hot as a vegetable course without the tomato sauce. In that case, oil a 6-cup soufflé mold and bake without the water bath. Serve in the baking pan. Serves 6.

Terrine de jambon aux courgettes

Ham and Zucchini Terrine

TRY TO BUY first-quality ham and imported Gouda for the best results. If you own a steel or plastic mandoline, you can easily slice the cheese. Otherwise, have it sliced at the cheese store.

SERVES 8 TO 10

2 medium zucchini, unpeeled, and cut in 1/8-inch slices (3 cups)

1 pound boiled ham, rind and fat discarded

1/4 pound lightly smoked ham, rind and fat discarded

2 eggs

1 large garlic clove

Freshly ground black pepper

7 ounces imported Gouda cheese, cut into thin slices

Bring several quarts of salted water to a boil. Add the zucchini and when the water comes back to a boil, cook for 2 minutes. Drain.

Preheat the oven to 350 degrees.

Oil a 6-cup loaf pan or terrine and place overlapping slices of zucchini on the sides and bottom of the pan. Refrigerate for 15 minutes.

Coarsely grind the hams in a food processor. Add eggs, garlic, and pepper; process until it makes a fine paste. You should have about 3 cups.

Place alternate layers of ham, Gouda, and the remaining zucchini slices in the loaf pan. Sprinkle with freshly ground pepper. (The ham mixture will probably provide enough salt.)

Tap the pan on the counter to pack it down; cover with a double layer of aluminum foil. Place the pan in a water bath and bake for 45 minutes.

Set aside to cool. Refrigerate at least 4 hours or overnight before unmolding.

To unmold: Warm the blade of a knife. Gently pass the warm blade between the pâté and the pan. Turn the pan over on a platter; hit the bottom of the pan with the handle of the knife, dislodging the pâté.

La Bavaroise aux poivrons rouges

Red Pepper Aspic

IN SUMMERTIME, when there is a special occasion to celebrate, I prepare this decorative first course. It takes time, but it can be prepared 3 to 4 days ahead of time.

SERVES 6

1/3 cup plus 2 tablespoons olive oil

4 pounds red bell peppers, quartered, seeds removed, and diced into 1/2-inch cubes (11 cups)

1 to 1 1/2 teaspoons salt

Pinch of cayenne

1 sprig of fresh thyme

1 cup Light Broth (page 11)

1 envelope unflavored gelatin

Fresh basil leaves (for garnish)

1 pound ripe fresh tomatoes, cored and quartered (2 cups)

1/2 teaspoon salt

In a 9-quart dutch oven, heat 1/3 cup oil. Stir in the pepper cubes, 1 teaspoon salt, cayenne pepper, and thyme. Cover and simmer, stirring occasionally, until very soft, about 1 hour.

Drain the peppers. (Reserve the liquid for the Red Pepper Soup, page 66.) Puree them in a food processor until smooth. You will have about 3 1/2 cups.

With the back of a large spoon, press the red pepper puree through a kitchen sieve to discard the skins.

Boil the light broth until it is reduced to 1/2 cup. Set aside to cool.

Sprinkle the gelatin over the cooled broth and whisk for 1 minute over medium high heat.

Whisk the broth into the red pepper puree. Taste and correct seasoning.

Oil six 1/2-cup ramekins or *darioles* for individual aspics or an 8-inch layer cake pan lined with oiled wax paper.

Pour the red pepper puree into the mold(s). Refrigerate overnight.

In the bowl of a food processor, process the tomatoes for 1 minute until smooth.

With the back of a large spoon, press the tomatoes through a kitchen sieve to discard the skins and seeds.

Sprinkle with ½ teaspoon salt. Refrigerate at least 30 minutes or up to 24 hours.

Run a knife around the inside of the ramekins or layer cake pan to loosen the aspic and invert onto individual plates or a serving platter.

Garnish with clusters of tiny basil leaves. Process the tomato sauce again in the food processor (the sauce separates in the refrigerator). Ladle fresh tomato sauce around the aspic(s) and fork in dribbles of the remaining olive oil.

Melon glacé au fromage blanc

Cold Honeydew with Fresh Cheese

TOWARD THE END of June, the famous cantaloupes of Cavaillon take over the fruit stands in the local markets, replacing strawberries and cherries. You never buy a cantaloupe without seeking the advice of the vendor, who swears to pick the best melon for you. I've been had many times, and since I can't tell the difference just by looking or smelling, I rely on the owner of a small supermarket in the charming village of Vinsobres, nearby, who is reputed to sell the best Cavaillons. We eat the sweet and refreshing melons almost every day, usually as a first course. Sometimes, when I have guests, I serve melon with goat cheese mixed with yogurt, mint, and lemon juice. In New York, I substitute honeydew melons, which are closer in sweetness to the Cavaillon melons than American cantaloupes.

SERVES 6

½ cup fresh ricotta cheese

½ cup drained plain yogurt

⅛ cup mint leaves

2 teaspoons lemon juice or more
    to taste

½ teaspoon salt

4 cups honeydew melon balls

6 small sprigs of mint leaves
    (for garnish)

Toasts (page 79)

In the bowl of a food processor, combine the ricotta with the yogurt, mint, lemon juice, and salt. Process until smooth. Taste and correct seasoning. Refrigerate several hours before serving.

Refrigerate the melon balls for 1 hour.

Arrange the melon balls on 6 plates. Dribble the cheese mixture over them just before serving and decorate each with a sprig of mint. Serve toasts on the side.

Rillettes au lapin

Shredded Rabbit Pâté

Rillettes IS A COUNTRY pâté made in many regions of France. The most famous *rillettes* are from Tours, on the Loire River, where the pâté is made of pork. In the southwest region of the Perigord and in the northeast region of Alsace, *rillettes* are made of goose or duck. In Provence, we make rabbit *rillettes*.

I have an unorthodox way of cooking the *rillettes*. Instead of cooking the meat in a very slow oven for many hours, I cook mine on top of the stove for about 2 hours or until the rabbit pieces are tender and start to caramelize in the fat. I like a slightly burned taste in the *rillettes*.

This is a perfect dish for holiday buffets. It's best if prepared many days ahead, but it is also good freshly made.

Several days before I intend to make *rillettes,* I ask my butcher in New York to save scraps of fat from pork roasts. Don't be alarmed by the amount of fat, the *rillettes* serve at least 20 people.

MAKES 1 QUART

One 3-pound rabbit, cut up

1 pound fresh pork fatback, ground

1 large onion, quartered

3 large garlic cloves, coarsely chopped

3 sprigs of fresh thyme

4 teaspoons salt

Freshly ground black pepper

½ pound lard (optional: for preserving the *rillettes*)

Salad greens (for garnish)

Small tart gherkins (cornichons) (for garnish)

Pearl Onion Relish (page 17) (for garnish)

In a 9-quart dutch oven, combine the rabbit, ground fat, onion, garlic, thyme, salt, pepper, and ½ cup water. Cover and cook for 2 to 3 hours on medium heat, turning the rabbit pieces over occasionally.

continued

When the meat starts to color and stick to the bottom of the pan, add another ¼ cup water and continue cooking until very tender, about 30 minutes.

Discard the thyme sprigs. Carefully bone the rabbit pieces.

In the bowl of a food processor, pulse the meat and fat in batches just until the meat is shredded.

Pack the *rillettes* in a 1-quart enamel terrine or glass loaf pan. Refrigerate until cold.

If you plan to keep the *rillettes* for more than 1 week, melt the lard and pour it over the cold *rillettes* to preserve them for about 3 months.

To serve: Take the *rillettes* out of the refrigerator at least 1 hour before serving. Scrape off the lard, if you've used it.

I like to unmold the *rillettes* onto a cutting board to make slicing easier. Decorate individual plates with salad greens. Make ¼-inch slices and place a slice of *rillettes* in the center of the greens; garnish with cornichons and pearl onion relish.

For a great sandwich, spread *rillettes* on potato bread and add lettuce.

VARIATION

Substitute 5-pound pork shoulder with bone for the rabbit.

Pâtes fraîches aux oeufs

Fresh Egg Pasta

IN MY KITCHEN, I made 1 batch of this pasta dough in a food processor and another I kneaded by hand. Both methods made good ravioli, but the hand technique produced a more tender pasta. It's up to you: it takes longer to make by hand, but it's very satisfying and it yields better, more tender ravioli.

MAKES 1 POUND DOUGH

2 cups unbleached all-purpose flour   ½ teaspoon salt

4 medium eggs, lightly beaten

THE HAND METHOD

On a pastry surface, make a 5-inch-wide well in the flour. Pour the beaten eggs and salt into the well. With a large fork, gradually incorporate the flour from the inside rim of the well until the eggs are no longer runny.

Start kneading the mixture with the palm of your hand until the mixture forms a dough. Stop for 15 minutes if it becomes difficult to knead more flour into the dough.

Sometimes the last of the flour to be kneaded is crumbly; sift it over the dough and discard the debris in the strainer.

With clean hands, continue kneading the dough with the palm of your hand until the flour is incorporated, folding and turning until the dough is very smooth (about 5 minutes).

Wrap the dough in plastic and set aside for 1 hour.

THE FOOD PROCESSOR METHOD

Process the flour, eggs, and salt until the dough forms a ball. Knead in more flour by hand if the dough is too sticky. Wrap in plastic and set aside for 1 hour.

Cut the dough into 2 pieces and flatten each piece. Sprinkle flour on each piece and fold into thirds like a business letter. Set the rollers of the pasta machine to the widest setting and pass the dough through, an open end feeding into the rollers. Repeat about 8 times, dusting flour, folding into thirds, and passing the dough through the widest setting until very smooth.

From then on, pass the dough only once (do not fold into thirds and dust flour only if the dough feels sticky) through each setting, up to the next to last.

The sheet of pasta will measure around 6 inches wide and 60 inches long. Cut it crosswise in 3 pieces.

For fettucine or angel hair, dry the pasta sheets before cutting them into the desired shape.

For ravioli, do not dry the pasta; quickly cut out the ravioli as directed in the ravioli recipes.

Pâtes fraîches aux truffes

Fresh Pasta with Truffles

HUNTING DOGS, shepherd dogs, truffle dogs, they all look alike in the Midi: friendly mongrels who don't look very smart. But I know not to be fooled by looks. I got to know Lulu, Belle, and Perlette, who were priceless in the eyes of their owners. Lulu was a savvy shepherdess; Belle and Perlette were ace truffle hunters. One Christmas Day, we spent the morning hunting truffles with Perlette. She sniffed the ground until she scented truffles, then tapped the ground with her paw several times, sat down and waited with anticipation for a lump of sugar, her reward for finding the truffle (when truffle dogs are trained, their reward is a truffle, but as they become seasoned truffle hunters, the reward is sugar). Truffles are a luxury everywhere and are eaten sparingly by all. Perlette was right every time. Belle was the saddest and mangiest-looking dog I have ever seen, but she was reputed to be the best truffle dog in Nyons. "See that dog?" a neighbor said to me when I was new in town. "She's the best truffle hunter in the region." "Yes, I know, and she lives next door to me!" For our first Christmas in Nyons, we ate truffles with pasta, thanks to Belle.

I buy truffles in small jars when Belle is not around to bring them to me.

SERVES 2

¼ pound black truffles, brushed under cold water and cut into ⅛-inch-thick slices when fresh; omit this step for canned truffles

3 tablespoons unsalted butter

2 tablespoons minced garlic

1 tablespoon marc, grappa, or brandy

½ batch Fresh Egg Pasta, cut into fettucine (page 31)

½ cup heavy cream

1 teaspoon salt

Freshly ground black pepper

In a medium saucepan, combine the truffles with butter, garlic, and marc, grappa, or brandy. Cover and braise over low heat for 15 minutes.

continued

In a large pan, bring several quarts of salted water to a boil. Add the pasta and once it comes back to the top in the boiling water, test for doneness. Cook to your taste. Drain.

In a large skillet, heat the cream over medium heat. Toss in the pasta and truffles, sprinkle with salt and pepper. Serve immediately.

Ravioles de Romans

Fresh Cheese Ravioli

ROMANS, THE CAPITAL of the shoe industry, is situated just north of Valence and is famous for ravioli stuffed with white cheese and herbs. Making ravioli takes time, but they can be made in several stages and frozen. At a dinner party in Romans, I met one of the managers of the cheese factory, who would not divulge with what cheese the ravioli are stuffed. I told him, never mind, I'll make up my own version.

MAKES SIXTY 2½-INCH RAVIOLI; SERVES 8

FOR THE STUFFING

1¼ cups fresh ricotta cheese

1¼ cups grated Parmesan cheese

1¼ cups shredded mozzarella cheese

½ cup chopped chives

2 large garlic cloves, coarsely chopped

1 teaspoon salt

Freshly ground black pepper

1 recipe Fresh Egg Pasta (page 31)

4 cups tomato sauce (page 8 or page 10)

½ cup grated Gruyère or Parmesan cheese

In the bowl of a food processor, process the cheese, chives, garlic, salt, and pepper until smooth. Taste and correct seasoning. Refrigerate until ready to fill the ravioli.

Stamp 2½-inch circles out of the pasta sheets. Dry the leftovers for soups. Mound 2 teaspoons cheese stuffing on half the circles and cover them with the remaining halves. Tightly seal the edges with the back of the tines of a fork.

Transfer the ravioli to a tea towel sprinkled with cornmeal and cover them with a second towel.

In large skillets, bring salted water to a light boil and poach the ravioli in batches for 10 minutes. Drain on a rack.

Serve with reheated tomato sauce and cheese on the side. In Romans, only grated Gruyère is sprinkled on the ravioli.

SALADS

Salade verte aux croutons • 39
   (Green Salad with Croutons)

Salade de mâche et trevisse au fenouil et au fromage • 40
   (Mâche, Radicchio, Fennel, and Cheese Salad)

Salade verte aux picodons rôtis • 41
   (Green Salad with Roasted Chèvre)

Salade de haricots verts au fromage et aux olives • 43
   (Green Bean, Cheese, and Olive Salad)

Salade nyonsaise • 45
   (Green Bean, Chanterelle, Olive, and Lettuce Salad)

Salade de poivrons aux anchois • 47
   (Pepper and Anchovy Salad)

Salade de poivrons et de tomates • 48
   (Pepper and Tomato Salad)

Salade cuite, Tante Gil • 49
   (Braised Tomato and Red Pepper Salad)

Salade de pommes de terre, haricots verts, et champignons • 50
   (Potato Salad with Green Beans and Mushrooms)

I COULD LIVE ON SALADS and I do. Give me a salad anytime with freshly baked bread, cheese, and a glass or two of wine and I am satisfied. I am not alone, judging by the number of salad bars that have proliferated in supermarkets, cafeterias, and restaurants during the last 10 years.

During summer in the Midi, salad is served as a first course. It is usually garden-fresh greens tossed in a very garlicky vinaigrette—or simply served with a drizzle of fragrant, herb-infused olive oil. One of my favorite first courses is a green salad with homemade garlic-rubbed croutons, tossed in the salad at the last minute.

I make meals of composed salads, especially during the summer when there are so many varieties of greens, vegetables, and herbs. Fall brings all kinds of mushrooms; winter is the time for fennel; and in spring we start again with greens.

Salads lend themselves to leftover meats, but you just can't throw anything together and call it a salad. It can be ruined easily if the ingredients are not well balanced, if there is too much or too little dressing, or if it is poorly seasoned. The dressing has to be made with excellent oil and vinegar. Don't cheat on the quality—this is the time to use that very expensive oil or vinegar you bought on a vacation in Italy or France. I also make sure the greens are bone dry before tossing them in the salad bowl; otherwise the water in the greens will dilute the dressing. After the salad is tossed, I always taste it to decide if it is perfectly seasoned before it goes on the table.

Salade verte aux croutons

Green Salad with Croutons

MY FAVORITE TOSSED green salad is deceptively simple. The croutons have to be just right, neither burned nor oily. There should be just a hint of garlic on each crouton, and they should be prepared at the last minute.

SERVES 6

Several 1-inch-thick slices of bread

6 tablespoons olive oil

1 tablespoon red wine vinegar

½ to 1 teaspoon salt

Freshly ground black pepper

1 large garlic clove, peeled

½ pound salad greens, washed and spun dry

1 tablespoon minced chives or 1 tablespoon minced fresh tarragon

Preheat the oven to 300 degrees.

Dry the bread slices in the oven for 10 minutes or until the bread surface is dry.

Meanwhile, in a large salad bowl, combine 4 tablespoons olive oil with the vinegar, salt, and freshly ground pepper. Set aside.

With a serrated knife, cut the bread into 1-inch cubes. You should have 3 cups of croutons. Place once more in the oven to dry the newly cut surfaces of the croutons. This step is important; if the bread surface is not dry, the croutons will absorb too much oil and become greasy.

In a large nonstick skillet, heat 2 tablespoons olive oil over medium heat. Brown the croutons lightly, turning them constantly.

Rub a cut garlic clove on the hot croutons.

Toss the salad greens and chives in the oil and vinegar dressing. Taste and correct seasoning.

Toss in the croutons last. Serve immediately.

Salade de mâche et trevisse au fenouil
et au fromage

Mâche, Radicchio, Fennel, and Cheese Salad

IN WINTER, WHEN I entertain, I serve this tossed salad, sometimes as a first course, and sometimes after the main dish in lieu of a cheese platter.

Mâche (lamb's tongue) is a green that needs to be washed several times, for sand sticks to it and is difficult to dislodge. I always pick a small head of radicchio, as the leaves near the core are more tender. Substitute other salad greens if mâche and radicchio are not available.

SERVES 4 TO 6

¼ pound mâche
   (lamb's tongue)

¼ pound radicchio

⅓ cup olive oil

2 tablespoons red wine vinegar

1 teaspoon fresh thyme leaves

½ to 1 teaspoon salt

Freshly ground black pepper

½ cup finely diced celery

3 tablespoons minced shallots

1 cup thinly sliced fennel strips

½ cup thinly sliced Gruyère strips

½ cup peeled tangerine or
   orange slices

Plunge the mâche in a large bowl of cold water and slosh it around well. Set aside for a minute. Repeat 2 or 3 times until the water is clear and there is no sand left at the bottom of the bowl. Spin dry.

Pick out the smallest and prettiest leaves of the radicchio. Wash and spin dry.

In a large salad bowl, combine the oil with the vinegar, thyme, salt, and freshly ground pepper.

Toss the mâche and radicchio in the salad bowl with the vinegar and oil dressing. Toss in the celery, shallots, fennel, cheese, and oranges. Taste and correct seasoning. Serve immediately.

Salade verte aux picodons rôtis

Green Salad with Roasted Chèvre

IN NYONS, every Thursday at the weekly market, I buy picodons, the goat cheese of the region made in Condorcet, a small village in the hills. There are many other goat cheese vendors at the market, but I like the cleanliness of the Condorcet stand and the cheese lady always wears an immaculate white uniform, which inspires confidence. Her display is simple: the one-day-old cheese, fresh curds, sold in faisselles (small cups with holes to drain the whey); the 3-day-old cheese, a soft white disk; the 1-week-old cheese, which gets dry and starts to form a greenish skin; and the 2- or 3-month-old cheese, a smaller disk, very hard and very pungent. My favorite for this salad is the 1-week-old picodon. It has lots of flavor without being overwhelming. In New York, I substitute imported Montrachet, which I cut into ½-inch-thick slices that resemble as much as possible my picodons of Condorcet.

SERVES 8

One 11-ounce cold Montrachet goat cheese, sliced into eight ¹/₂-inch-thick slices

1 teaspoon salt

Freshly ground black pepper

6 tablespoons olive oil

1 egg, beaten

1 cup coarse homemade bread crumbs

1 tablespoon red wine vinegar

2 tablespoons plain yogurt

1 teaspoon minced fresh tarragon

¹/₄ pound arugula, large stems removed

¹/₂ pound red leaf lettuce

Sprinkle the cheese with ½ teaspoon salt and freshly ground pepper.

In a large nonstick skillet, heat 2 tablespoons oil over medium heat.

Quickly dip the cheese first in the beaten egg, then in the bread crumbs. Fry the goat cheese, turning it over once until golden brown, about 5 minutes. The cheese should be slightly melted inside and crisp on the outside (the domestic Montrachet takes longer to melt than the softer French Montrachet).

continued

In a large mixing bowl, whisk the vinegar with the remaining olive oil, yogurt, and tarragon. Sprinkle with ½ teaspoon salt and freshly ground pepper.

Toss the salad greens in the dressing. Taste and correct seasoning.

Serve the salad on individual plates with the fried chèvre on top.

Salade de haricots verts au fromage
et aux olives

Green Bean, Cheese, and Olive Salad

I AM NOT a gardener but I have the luck to live next to one who lets me pick all the vegetables I want. But we do not agree on green beans; he likes his beans large and mature and I like to pick them when they are small and very tender (*haricots verts fins*). We've come to an agreement. I have my patch and he has his (he takes care of both).

For a period of about 2 weeks when the beans are ready, I could turn into a bean, eating this salad every day. My husband is not very fond of green beans (he prefers white beans), so I entertain at lunch. My friend Patti Hart from Arizona, who tested most of these recipes, became lyrical and had this to say: "This is my kind of recipe—fast, beautiful, and divine!"

I pay attention when the beans are cooking, testing them constantly to be sure to have just the right doneness, neither raw nor overdone.

SERVES 6

1 teaspoon mustard

4 teaspoons red wine vinegar

5 tablespoons olive oil

1 to 1½ teaspoons salt

2 pounds young green beans or *haricots verts*, ends cut off

⅓ cup minced parsley

2 large garlic cloves, minced

½ cup grated Gruyère or Parmesan cheese

⅔ cup Niçoise or Gaeta olives

Freshly ground black pepper

In a large mixing bowl, combine mustard, vinegar, oil, and 1 teaspoon salt.

Sort the beans by thickness, making several separate piles.

In a large pan, bring several quarts of salted water to a boil. Plunge the thickest beans in the boiling water first. Count 1 minute after the water boils again and add the smaller beans in turn. Boil the beans until just cooked through but still crisp.

continued

Drain the beans well and quickly toss them in the vinegar and oil dressing with the parsley and garlic.

Sprinkle the cheese and black olives over the beans. Correct seasoning with the remaining salt and freshly ground pepper.

Salade nyonsaise

Green Bean, Chanterelle, Olive, and Lettuce Salad

IN NORTHERN PROVENCE, around the third week of August when the hot dry spell is over for the summer, we get tremendous short thunderstorms. That's when I start looking in the market for the Ardéchois, my mushroom man. He comes every Thursday and Sunday to the Nyons market from the Ardèche region, just west of the Rhone. He is the first to sell chanterelles. The price is high, but they are such a prize that I pay it willingly. I know that those mushrooms have been freshly picked because I generally have to pick out strands of green moss still clinging to them. I buy a small amount and mix the mushrooms with young green beans or *haricots verts* and salad greens.

Substitute shiitake mushrooms or any other mushroom in lieu of chanterelles if you wish. I sprinkle on ½ cup of Nyons olives at the last minute and in New York I substitute Niçoise or Gaeta olives.

SERVES 4 TO 6

6 tablespoons olive oil

1 tablespoon red wine vinegar

½ to 1 teaspoon salt

Freshly ground black pepper

¾ pound young green beans or *haricots verts*, ends cut off

¼ pound chanterelle mushrooms, wiped cleaned and quartered

1 large garlic clove, minced

½ pound red oak leaf lettuce, washed and spun dry

½ cup shredded basil leaves

½ cup Niçoise or Gaeta olives

In a large salad bowl, combine 4 tablespoons olive oil with the vinegar, salt, and freshly ground pepper. Set aside.

In a large pan, bring 3 quarts of salted water to a boil. Add the beans and boil until just cooked through but still crisp, 3 to 4 minutes. Drain well and toss in the oil and vinegar dressing. continued

In a nonstick skillet, heat 2 tablespoons olive oil over medium high heat. Stir fry the chanterelles, shaking the pan occasionally, for about 2 to 3 minutes. Add garlic and cook for 1 minute, shaking the pan to avoid burning the garlic. Toss the chanterelles with the green beans or *haricots verts*.

Toss the salad leaves and basil with the mushrooms and green beans. Sprinkle the olives on top and serve.

Salade de poivrons aux anchois

Pepper and Anchovy Salad

ANCHOVIES ARE A staple of my French kitchen, but I have many friends who are not as fond of them as I am, especially in the States. Even in New York City, it is difficult to find freshly salted anchovies. I always substitute anchovies canned in oil or if I find small sardines in brine, I'll buy them. You can make this pepper salad without the anchovies or sardines; it is still very good.

SERVES 6

6 red bell peppers

4 yellow bell peppers

6 anchovy fillets, drained
 and patted dry

$\frac{1}{2}$ to 1 teaspoon salt

2 large garlic cloves, minced

2 tablespoons red wine vinegar

6 tablespoons olive oil

10 scallions, finely cut

Char the peppers over a gas flame, turning occasionally. For an electric stove, set the broiler on high for 5 minutes. Place the peppers 4 inches under the heating element and broil until completely charred, turning every 5 minutes. Alternatively, charcoal on a barbecue over very hot coals. Place them in a sturdy plastic bag and set aside until cool.

Cut the anchovy fillets in half lengthwise.

In a mixing bowl, combine salt, garlic, vinegar, and oil. Set aside.

Peel the peppers and discard the stem ends. Quarter them and remove the seeds. Strain the pepper juices.

On a decorative platter, overlap the peppers in alternating colors and spoon the pepper juices over. Crisscross the anchovy fillets on top of the peppers and scatter the scallions around the peppers. Dribble the oil and vinegar dressing over the peppers and scallions.

Salade de poivrons et de tomates

Pepper and Tomato Salad

I PLAN SEVERAL meals around this salad. One day, I serve it with a roast; another day, I pour it over hot pasta or I serve it with steamed potatoes and a tossed green salad.

SERVES 10

4 red bell peppers

4 yellow bell peppers

4½ pounds fresh tomatoes, peeled, seeded, and coarsely chopped (8 to 9 cups) (see Note, page 9)

1½ teaspoons salt or more

½ cup basil leaves

4 large garlic cloves, coarsely chopped

⅓ cup olive oil

Char the peppers (see preceding recipe) and place them in a sturdy plastic bag; set aside until cool.

Place the chopped tomatoes in a kitchen strainer over a bowl. Sprinkle with 1 teaspoon salt and drain for ½ hour.

Peel and quarter the peppers; discard stems and seeds. Cut each quarter into 3 pieces crosswise.

In a large bowl toss the peppers with the drained tomatoes.

In the bowl of a food processor, process basil, garlic, and ½ teaspoon salt for 1 minute, stopping once or twice to scrape the sides of the bowl. With the motor running, dribble the oil through the chute.

Pour the basil dressing over the peppers and tomatoes and mix thoroughly. Taste and correct seasoning. Refrigerate overnight; the more it marinates in the refrigerator, the better it gets.

Remove from the refrigerator at least 1 hour before dinner to serve at room temperature.

Salade cuite, Tante Gil

Braised Tomato and Red Pepper Salad

GILBERTE GUÉRON, who owns a house not very far from mine in the Drôme hills, brought this salad back from Algeria. Tante Gil (as she is called) taught me to make this salad in her kitchen, and for years now I have made batches of it every summer and kept it for weeks in the refrigerator. It also freezes well for winter days when you can't live without peppers and tomatoes. Serve the salad with broiled chicken or guinea hens (page 131) or over pasta.

MAKES 8 CUPS

4 pounds red bell peppers

$^{1}/_{2}$ cup olive oil

4 pounds fresh tomatoes, peeled, seeded, and chopped (8 cups) (see Note, page 9)

6 large garlic cloves, peeled and quartered ($^{1}/_{3}$ cup)

2 teaspoons salt

$^{1}/_{8}$ teaspoon cayenne

1 teaspoon fresh thyme leaves

Preset the broiler to high.

Broil the peppers on a cookie sheet lined with aluminum foil, turning them over until they are evenly charred. Place them in a sturdy plastic bag and set aside to cool.

In a 6-quart dutch oven, heat the oil over medium heat. Stir in the tomatoes, garlic, salt, cayenne pepper, and thyme. Cover and simmer over medium heat for 20 minutes.

Peel the peppers and discard the stems. Quarter, seed, and core the peppers. Chop coarsely. Yields about 6 cups.

Add the peppers to the tomatoes. Cover and simmer 20 minutes over medium heat.

Over high heat, uncover and cook until the tomato and pepper juices have evaporated, stirring frequently, about 30 minutes. Correct seasoning.

Serve hot as a vegetable, cold for a salad.

Salade de pommes de terre, haricots verts, et champignons

Potato Salad with Green Beans and Mushrooms

THROUGHOUT THE YEAR, my husband and I eat a variety of salads for dinner. Many times, the salad consists of greens and whatever is left over from my classes. In the summer I often mix new potatoes and green beans with mushrooms. I add a small amount of lean bacon or leftover meat when the salad is our meal.

In Nyons, I choose the prized French potatoes, the Rattes, and in the States, fingerling potatoes or small red-skinned potatoes. As much as I like the skin of baked potatoes, I am not fond of new potato skins—they are too thin and too papery, but it's a matter of taste.

SERVES 2 FOR DINNER; 4 TO 6
FOR A FIRST COURSE

1^{1}/$_{4}$ pounds fingerling (Ruby Crescent, Irene, or Ratte) potatoes, scrubbed under running cold water

5 tablespoons olive oil

1 tablespoon red wine vinegar

1 teaspoon salt

Freshly ground black pepper

4 ounces lean bacon, cut into strips ^{1}/$_{3}$ inch wide and 1^{1}/$_{2}$ inches long (1 cup)

6 ounces mushrooms, stems trimmed, caps and stems quartered (1 cup)

2 garlic cloves, thinly sliced

^{3}/$_{4}$ pound young green beans or *haricots verts*, ends cut

^{1}/$_{4}$ cup shredded basil leaves

In a large pan, cover the potatoes with salted cold water. Bring to a boil and simmer until tender, about 15 to 20 minutes.

Meanwhile, in a salad bowl, combine 4 tablespoons olive oil with the vinegar, salt, and freshly ground pepper.

Drain the potatoes. Peel and quarter. Toss them quickly in the dressing.

In a nonstick skillet, heat 1 teaspoon olive oil and stir fry the bacon for 5 minutes. Discard the fat. Toss the bacon with the potatoes.

Add 2 teaspoons olive oil to the skillet and briefly stir fry the mushrooms, shaking the pan occasionally, until lightly browned, about 2 minutes. Add garlic and cook for 1 minute, shaking the pan to avoid burning the garlic. Toss the mushrooms with the potatoes and bacon.

In a large pan, bring 3 quarts of salted water to a boil. Add the beans and boil until just cooked through but still crisp, 3 to 4 minutes. Drain and toss the beans and basil with the potatoes.

Taste and correct seasoning. Serve immediately.

Salade de carottes râpées

Grated Carrot Salad

EVERY 2 WEEKS or so, I crave grated carrots. I find there's always a catch to simple and easy recipes; for this one, the carrots taste better if they are finely grated.

SERVES 4

1 pound carrots, peeled

½ teaspoon salt

1 tablespoon red wine vinegar

4 tablespoons olive oil

1 teaspoon dry oregano

Freshly ground black pepper

Grate the carrots using the fine shredder of a food processor, the medium shredder of a Mouli-julienne, or a hand grater (yields 3 cups).

In a salad bowl, whisk salt, vinegar, oil, and oregano. Toss in the shredded carrots and grind pepper over them; mix well and taste. Add more salt and pepper if you wish.

Salade de pâtes fraîches aux herbes

Fresh Pasta Salad

YEARS AGO I tossed this green herb dressing in pasta for Alice and Calvin Trillin in their rented house in St. Remy de Provence. You should add as much garlic as you like–Bud Trillin can never get enough!

I serve this herb vinaigrette with dishes other than pasta; it's perfect for poached or grilled fish, steamed new potatoes, cold chicken, etc.

SERVES 8

2 hard-boiled eggs

2 teaspoons Dijon mustard

1/4 cup chopped fresh chives

1/4 cup tarragon leaves

1/2 cup parsley leaves

4 large garlic cloves, finely chopped

1 teaspoon salt

3 tablespoons red wine vinegar

3/4 cup olive oil

1 tablespoon drained capers

Fresh Egg Pasta, cut into fettucine or angel hair (page 31)

Freshly ground black pepper

Dice the cooked egg whites.

In the bowl of a food processor, process the egg yolks, mustard, herbs, garlic, and 1 teaspoon salt, occasionally scraping the work bowl. With the motor running, dribble the vinegar and oil through the chute.

Pour the dressing in a large bowl, add the capers and the egg whites. Set aside. In a large kettle, boil several quarts of salted water. Add the pasta and cook until *al dente,* about 1 minute.

Drain and toss the pasta in the dressing. Sprinkle with freshly ground pepper. Taste and correct seasoning.

Salade verte à la volaille et aux oranges

Green Salad with Duck Breast and Oranges

MY NUMEROUS SUMMER guests often bring Beaumes de Venise, a sweet wine made in the village of Beaumes de Venise about 30 miles south of Nyons. I made up this recipe to use the abundance of this delicious wine. In my New York kitchen, I substitute port.

When wine or liquor is used in cooking, bring to a boil and light a match to it to burn off the alcohol.

SERVES 8

2 duck breasts (about 2 pounds), fat trimmed off	1 teaspoon fresh thyme leaves
2 teaspoons salt	$^2/_3$ cup tawny port or Beaumes de Venise
Freshly ground black pepper	$^1/_2$ pound arugula
4 seedless oranges	$^1/_2$ pound red oak leaf lettuce
2 tablespoons red wine vinegar	2 shallots, minced
$^1/_3$ cup olive oil	$^1/_2$ cup diced celery

Place the duck breasts, skin side down, in a small roasting pan with low sides. Sprinkle with 1 teaspoon salt and freshly ground pepper. Set aside for 1 hour or refrigerate overnight; bring to room temperature before cooking.

Preheat the oven to 425 degrees.

With a serrated knife, using sawlike motions, cut off the skin and white pith of the oranges to expose the flesh. Slice off and discard the skin that separates the orange wedges. Set aside.

In a large mixing bowl, mix the vinegar, oil, thyme, 1 teaspoon salt, and freshly ground pepper. Set aside.

Roast the duck breasts on the middle rack of the oven for 10 minutes for medium rare. Set aside for 5 minutes on a cutting board.

Discard the fat in the pan and pour in the port. Heat the port, scraping the bottom of the pan to release the drippings. Strike a match and flambé the port. Set aside.

Remove the layer of fat and skin from the duck. Cut the duck breasts on a slant into ½-inch strips. Reheat the duck slices in the port for 1 minute.

Toss the salad greens in the bowl with the vinegar and oil dressing. Toss in the shallots, celery, and orange slices. Correct seasoning.

Serve the tossed salad on individual plates with the duck slices on top and dribble some port sauce over. Pour the remaining sauce in a sauceboat.

Salade de cocos aux scupions

Bean and Squid Salad

IN AUGUST, the French markets are full of the first freshly picked white beans, *cocos*. Besides making soupe au pistou, I toss them in salads. Substitute shrimp for squid if you prefer. In the States, you can buy fresh cranberry beans at the same time of year. If you can't find fresh beans, substitute dried ones.

This salad is better eaten the day after you prepare it, but remember to serve it at room temperature.

SERVES 6

1 pound dry cannellini or navy beans or 3 pounds cranberry beans in their pods, shelled (5 cups)

½ cup olive oil

2 onions, thinly sliced (2 cups)

4 large garlic cloves, coarsely chopped

2 pounds fresh tomatoes, peeled, seeded, and chopped (4 cups) (see Note, page 9)

3½ teaspoons salt

1 teaspoon mustard

1 tablespoon red wine vinegar

Freshly ground black pepper

½ cup thinly sliced shallots

¼ cup shredded fresh basil or ¼ cup shredded fresh mint

1 pound squid, cleaned

Soak dried beans overnight in cold water. Drain. Cover with more cold water and bring to a boil. Drain once more.

There is no need to soak and parboil the fresh beans.

In a 6-quart dutch oven, heat 3 tablespoons olive oil over medium heat. Add the onions and garlic. Cover and braise for 5 minutes.

Uncover, add the tomatoes, and cook for 5 minutes over medium high heat, stirring occasionally.

Add the beans and pour 3 cups cold water over them. Simmer over medium heat for 1 hour or until soft; stir occasionally. Sprinkle with 3 teaspoons salt after 30 minutes.

In a large salad bowl, combine the mustard with 4 tablespoons olive oil, vinegar, $1/4$ teaspoon salt, and freshly ground pepper. Set aside.

Drain the beans if necessary (keep the bean liquid for basting a roast or to add to a soup) and toss them in the oil and vinegar dressing with the shallots and basil.

Slice the squid into $1/2$-inch-thick rings and turn them inside out to clean thoroughly under cold running water.

In a nonstick skillet, heat 1 tablespoon olive oil over medium high heat and stir fry the squids for 1 minute or until they lightly color. Sprinkle with $1/4$ teaspoon salt.

Toss the squid with the beans. Cover and set aside at least 4 hours to blend the flavors before serving; or refrigerate overnight but bring to room temperature before serving.

Soups

"*L*ydie, *mange ta soupe!*" Every night of my childhood I heard this demand. We had soup because it fills you up at the start of a meal. My mother's childhood in a peasant household in the hills of northern Provence got her into the habit of eating soup and she never got over it. Luckily, she knew how to make good robust soups with the meager ingredients available during and just after World War II. When I married a soup fanatic, I was well armed. Wayne actually sold his vote for soup. He voted for my preferred presidential candidate (who won) in exchange for soup on demand for the next four years!

All over France, vegetable soups are still served in farmhouses for *soupers* every day. Vegetable soups are generally made with water and first-quality produce.

Most of the soups in this chapter are made not with vegetable broth but with a light chicken broth because the vegetables in the States are less flavorful than those I buy in France. When I don't have a light broth handy, I make soup with water and chicken parts. When the soup is ready, I bone the chicken meat and reserve it for sandwiches or for the large salads that we frequently eat.

Try to be seasonal; remember a fresh tomato soup can be splendid in August but not in January.

Bouillabaisse d'asperges

Asparagus Bouillabaisse

TRADITIONALLY, ASPARAGUS BOUILLABAISSE is cooked in garlicky boiling water with a potato. At the last minute, eggs are poached in the broth. At home, in my New York kitchen, I cook the asparagus in a velouté based on olive oil, flour, and light broth, and I pass along a bowl of aioli (garlic mayonnaise) at the table.

SERVES 8

3 tablespoons olive oil

3 tablespoons flour

6 cups boiling Light Broth
    (page 11)

3 pounds asparagus, tough ends
    removed, and cut crosswise
    into halves

1 sprig of fresh sage

2 teaspoons salt

Toasts (page 79)

Aioli (page 104)

In a large pan, heat the oil, whisk in the flour until the mixture is smooth, and whisk in the boiling stock.

Bring again to a boil and add the asparagus stalks, sage, and salt (adjusted to account for the saltiness of commercial chicken stock if you do not make your own).

Cover and simmer for 30 minutes.

In a food processor, puree the soup in batches. Taste and correct seasoning.

Reheat the soup. Serve toasts and aioli on the side. Each guest swirls a scoop of aioli in the bouillabaisse or spreads it on toast and adds that to the soup.

Bouillabaisse aux épinards

Spinach Bouillabaisse

IN THE MIDI I heard that ladies wash their tile floors with the water in which spinach parboiled. Of course, I had to try it. I still like liquid wax for my floor!

What we call California spinach in the eastern United States is young tender spinach.

SERVES 8

$2\frac{1}{2}$ pounds California spinach, washed and stems removed

5 tablespoons olive oil

1 large onion, thinly sliced (2 cups)

4 garlic cloves, peeled and coarsely chopped

$\frac{1}{2}$ pound russet potato, peeled and cut into $\frac{1}{2}$-inch cubes (1 cup)

2 teaspoons salt

Freshly ground black pepper

3 tablespoons flour

6 cups Light Broth (page 11)

Aioli (page 104)

Toasts (page 79)

In a large kettle, bring several quarts of salted water to a boil. Plunge the spinach in the boiling water and bring back to a boil. Boil 2 minutes and drain. Rinse under cold water, then squeeze out the water and chop coarsely. Set aside.

In a large skillet, heat 2 tablespoons olive oil over medium heat. Add the onion, garlic, spinach, and potato. Sprinkle with $\frac{1}{2}$ teaspoon salt and freshly ground pepper. Cook over medium heat for 5 minutes, stirring occasionally.

In a large pan, heat the remaining olive oil and whisk in the flour until smooth. Pour in the chicken broth and the vegetables. Sprinkle with $1\frac{1}{2}$ teaspoons salt and freshly ground pepper. Cover and simmer for 30 minutes.

Taste and correct seasoning. Serve with aioli and toasts.

Soupe aux carottes

Carrot Soup

IN LATE SUMMER, my neighbors give me garden fresh carrots with which I make this soup and eat it cold. In wintertime, I serve it hot.

SERVES 8

3 tablespoons olive oil

1 medium onion, chopped coarsely (1 cup)

1 tablespoon minced garlic

1½ pounds carrots, cut into ⅛-inch-thick slices (5 cups)

1½ pounds fresh tomatoes, peeled, seeded, and chopped (3½ cups) (see Note, page 9) or one 35-ounce can plum tomatoes, drained

½ cup basil leaves

2 teaspoons salt

Freshly ground black pepper

5 cups Light Broth (page 11)

In a 6-quart dutch oven, heat the oil over medium heat. Add the onions and garlic and cook for 5 minutes, stirring occasionally.

Add the carrots, tomatoes, and basil. Sprinkle with salt and freshly ground pepper. Cover and cook over medium heat for 15 minutes.

Add the broth, cover, and simmer for 1 hour or until the carrots are very tender.

Puree the soup in several batches in the food processor until smooth. Taste and correct seasoning.

Serve hot or cold.

Soupe à la coucourde

Pumpkin Soup

Coucourde IS THE Provençal word for pumpkin and in the southern tip of the Drôme, there is a small town called Coucourde that celebrates the *coucourdes* harvest in October. In the region, markets sell wedges of pumpkin. In the States, I use 1 pumpkin for several quarts of soup, which is good hot or cold.

MAKES 3 QUARTS

3 tablespoons olive oil

4 medium onions, coarsely chopped (4 cups)

4 large garlic cloves, minced (4 teaspoons)

6 pounds pumpkin flesh, peeled, seeded, and cut into 1-inch cubes (9 cups)

1 pound russet potatoes, cut into 1-inch cubes (2 cups)

¼ cup minced fresh tarragon (substitute fresh parsley if tarragon is unavailable)

2 tablespoons salt

Freshly ground black pepper

10 cups Light Broth (page 11)

Sour cream (for garnish)

In a 9-quart dutch oven, heat the oil over medium heat. Add the onions and garlic; cook for 5 minutes, stirring occasionally.

Add the pumpkin, potatoes, and tarragon, and sprinkle with salt and freshly ground pepper. Cover and cook over medium heat for 10 minutes.

Pour in the broth, cover, and simmer for 45 minutes, or until the pumpkin is tender.

In a food processor, puree the soup in batches until smooth. Taste and correct seasoning.

Dribble sour cream on top of the hot soup and serve.

Soupe aux tomates fraîches

Fresh Tomato Soup

I MAKE THIS soup only in August, at the peak of the tomato season. The lemon juice in the soup brings out the flavor of the very ripe and sweet tomatoes. Serve it very cold with Tapenade (page 19) or Eggplant Caviar (page 18) spread on toasts.

SERVES 6

4 pounds very ripe fresh tomatoes, coarsely chopped (8 cups)

2 tablespoons freshly squeezed lemon juice

1 tablespoon salt

½ cup sour cream (for garnish)

Small clusters of fresh mint leaves (for garnish)

In a food processor, puree the tomatoes in batches for 1 minute.

Force the puree through a kitchen strainer, pushing on the solids with the back of a large spoon to extract the pulp and juices. Discard the skins and seeds that remain in the strainer.

Gradually season the tomato soup with lemon juice, and with salt until it is adjusted to your taste.

Refrigerate for several hours or a day.

Puree the soup once more in the food processor before serving (the pulp and liquid will separate in the refrigerator). Taste and correct seasoning (more salt and lemon juice might be necessary).

Season the sour cream with ¼ teaspoon salt.

Pour the soup into individual soup plates. Garnish with 1 tablespoon sour cream and a cluster of mint leaves.

Soupe aux poivrons rouges

Red Pepper Soup

SERVES 8

⅓ cup olive oil

4 pounds red bell peppers, quartered, seeds and piths removed, and diced into ½-inch cubes (11 cups)

1 pound potatoes, cut into ½-inch cubes (2 cups)

1 medium onion, sliced (1 cup)

1½ teaspoons salt

Pinch of cayenne

1 sprig of fresh thyme or 1 teaspoon dry thyme

2 cups Light Broth (page 11)

Sour cream (for garnish)

Small basil leaves (for garnish)

In a 9-quart dutch oven, heat the oil over medium high heat. Stir in the peppers, potatoes, onions, salt, cayenne, and thyme. Cover and simmer, stirring occasionally, until very soft, about 1 hour.

Drain the vegetables and set aside the liquid. In a food processor, puree the peppers and potatoes in batches until smooth.

Strain the puree through a kitchen sieve; discard the skins.

Combine the vegetables, the reserved liquid, and broth in a large pot; bring to a boil.

To serve hot, dribble sour cream on top of the soup and garnish with the basil leaves.

To serve cold, cool the soup and refrigerate for several hours. Garnish as the hot soup.

Soupe aux cèpes

Porcini Soup

MANY OF MY neighbors in Nyons are self-educated mycologists and in early mornings of October, they go out surreptitiously to their favorite spots looking for wild mushrooms. *Cèpes* (porcini) are the most common wild mushrooms in our northern Provençal hills. Instead of fresh *cèpes*, which would be too expensive in New York, I buy them dry and cook them with cultivated mushrooms. In markets around New York, I found that buying dry *cèpes* under their Italian name (porcini) is cheaper than under their French name (*cèpes*).

SERVES 8

2 ounces dried porcini (1 cup)

3 tablespoons olive oil

3 medium onions, coarsely chopped (3 cups)

2 large garlic cloves, minced

1 pound cultivated white mushrooms

⅓ cup minced parsley

2 teaspoons salt or more

5 cups Light Broth (page 11)

Freshly ground black pepper

3 tablespoons sour cream (for garnish)

Small flat parsley leaves (for garnish)

Put the porcini in a strainer and scrub them under cold water to remove sand. Soak them in 2 cups warm water for 2 hours. Strain through cheesecloth, reserving the liquid. Coarsely chop the porcini and set aside.

Reduce the porcini liquid at a steady boil to 1 cup.

In a 6-quart dutch oven, heat the olive oil. Add the onions and garlic. Cover and cook over medium heat for 5 minutes. Add the cultivated mushrooms, the minced parsley, and 1 teaspoon salt. Cover and simmer for 15 minutes.

Add the reserved porcini, the reduced liquid, and the light broth. Sprinkle with 1 teaspoon salt and freshly ground pepper and bring to a boil. Lower the heat, cover, and simmer for 35 minutes.

Taste and correct seasoning. Serve the soup in individual plates. Garnish with a teaspoon of sour cream and small flat parsley leaves.

Soupe au pistou à ma façon

Soup of Fresh Cranberry Beans with Tomatoes and Basil

WHEN FRESH *cocos* (white beans) appear on the stands of French markets in August, it's time for me to make my favorite summer soup—pistou. In the Midi, basil is called *pistou,* but it also means a mixture of basil, cheese, olive oil, and garlic.

SERVES 6

⅓ cup olive oil

2 onions, thinly sliced (2 cups)

2 pounds fresh tomatoes, peeled, seeded, and chopped (4 cups) (see Note, page 9)

3 pounds cranberry beans in the pod, shelled (5 cups) or 2 cups dry cannellini, navy, or Great Northern beans

1 tablespoon salt

1 cup shredded fresh basil leaves

6 large garlic cloves, minced

2 cups freshly grated Gruyère cheese

In a 6-quart dutch oven, heat the oil on medium high heat. Stir in the onion, cover, lower the heat, and braise for 10 minutes.

Stir in the tomatoes. Cover and braise for 10 minutes.

Add the beans and pour 4 cups water over them. Cover and cook over medium heat for 1 hour or until the beans are tender. After 30 minutes, add the salt.

Add the basil and garlic and cook for another 2 to 3 minutes.

Serve hot with freshly grated Gruyère.

NOTE:

To make the soup with dried beans, soak 2 cups dried cannellini, navy, or Great Northern beans overnight in cold water.

Drain the beans. In a 6-quart dutch oven cover the beans with cold water. Bring to a boil and drain.

Proceed with the above recipe.

Consommé à l'estragon

Consommé with Fresh Tarragon

TO MAKE A clear consommé, I clarify my light broth with a thick blanket of egg whites. The whites act as a magnet, pulling to the surface all the impurities in the broth. I find that a tall narrow pot is essential for successful clarification. The egg whites must form a very thick surface, which is difficult to achieve if the surface of the pan is very wide.

SERVES 6

1 cup minced parsley

2 cloves

2 peppercorns

3 egg whites, slightly beaten

3 egg shells, crumbled

4 cups cold degreased Light Broth (page 11)

2 sprigs of fresh tarragon

Toasts (page 79)

1 cup freshly grated Parmesan cheese

In a deep narrow pot (8 inches wide, 6 inches deep), combine the parsley, cloves, peppercorns, egg whites, and egg shells. Pour in the cold chicken broth over it.

Over medium heat, whisk constantly until the broth comes to a boil (about 15 minutes). This is the most important step, the egg whites must become very thick and frothy.

Lower the heat to medium low and cook for 15 to 20 minutes. The egg whites will turn grayish and form a thick blanket and they should not disintegrate in the soup, which will happen if the broth starts boiling.

Strain the consommé through several layers of damp cheesecloth without disturbing the thick blanket of egg whites in the pan.

Discard the egg whites and clean the pot before reheating the consommé with the tarragon. Turn off the heat, cover, and set aside for 30 minutes.

Reheat the consommé and discard the tarragon.

Serve with toasts and a bowl of freshly grated Parmesan.

Soupe aux lentilles vertes

Lentil Soup

GREEN LENTILS, UNLIKE brown or yellow lentils, keep their shape when cooked. Lentil soup is our Christmas Eve supper at the château in Nyons. Wayne prepares the lentils and I make the broth for the soup several days ahead. We generally start with oysters on the half-shell; the lentil soup follows with freshly baked baguettes (page 78) and we drink a Chardonnay from St. Jalle, a village near Nyons.

One pound of lentils makes a lot of soup, so reserve some of the lentils for a salad if you like. The ratio of broth to lentils is one to one: that is, 1 cup of cooked lentils with meat to 1 cup of broth. The soup can be prepared several days ahead of time.

SERVES 10

$\frac{1}{4}$ cup olive oil

1 pound lean pork chop, boned and cut into $\frac{1}{2}$-cubes (about 2 cups), bone reserved

4 ounces Canadian bacon, diced into $\frac{1}{2}$-inch cubes ($\frac{2}{3}$ cup)

4 ounces chorizo, diced into $\frac{1}{2}$-inch cubes ($\frac{2}{3}$ cup)

3 large carrots, diced into $\frac{1}{2}$-inch cubes (1$\frac{1}{2}$ cups)

2 medium onions, coarsely chopped (2 cups)

2 large leeks, white parts only, coarsely chopped (2 cups)

3 large garlic cloves, coarsely chopped

1 sprig of fresh thyme or 1 teaspoon dry thyme

10 peppercorns

1 pound green lentils, rinsed

1$\frac{1}{2}$ to 2 teaspoons salt

8 cups Light Broth (page 11)

In a 9-quart dutch oven, heat the oil and sauté, stirring, the pork, pork bone, bacon, and chorizo for 3 minutes.

Add the carrots, onions, leeks, and garlic. Sauté 2 to 3 minutes. Add the thyme, peppercorns, and 2 cups water. Cover, lower the heat, and simmer for 15 minutes.

Stir in the lentils. Sprinkle with 1½ teaspoons salt; add 3 more cups of water.

Cover tightly and simmer for 1 hour or until the lentils are tender.

Discard the pork bone. Add the broth and reheat. Taste and add more salt if necessary.

VARIATION

Salade de lentilles

LENTIL SALAD

¼ teaspoon salt

Freshly ground black pepper

2 teaspoons red wine vinegar

3 tablespoons olive oil

2 cups cooked lentils

In a bowl, combine salt, pepper, vinegar, and oil. Toss in the lentils. Taste and correct seasoning.

Around a Pissaladière

Pissaladière, the Provençal version of pizza, originated in Nice and now is served all over Provence.

The classic topping for a pissaladière is an onion and anchovy marmalade with olives strewn on top. The dough is a thick bready crust more like Sicilian pizza than thin-crust pizzas. Today, the imaginative cook concocts toppings according to whim, the availability of produce, or leftovers in the refrigerator. The bready dough is sometimes replaced by pastry dough, but the toppings are interchangeable. I alternate between the two types, favoring short crust pastry (*pâte brisée*) when I am serving savory tarts as appetizers for a dinner party. I prefer bready-crust pissaladières as a main dish with a tossed green salad for family dinners.

My friends and neighbors in the Midi buy bread dough at their bakery when they feel like making a pissaladière and are always amazed about how much better mine tastes. A teacher can't stop teaching; I show them how to make potato bread dough that is not at all Provençal but adapts itself beautifully to a pissaladière or a fougasse.

I have always been partial to potato bread. I ate it for the first time in Ohio when I had just arrived from France in 1953. During World War II, I had eaten corn bread made from fodder corn, so you can imagine how much better potato bread was; it was food from heaven for a fifteen-year-old! Many years later, when writing a book on potatoes, I hunted and hunted for the best potato bread recipe. I found it in Elizabeth

David's book on bread. It was written by Eliza Acton, a nineteenth-century cookbook author. The recipe called for 7 pounds of potatoes and 7 pounds of flour. I played in my kitchen, reducing it to manageable proportions. I can say that this is my favorite recipe of all. It's easy to make, it's cheap, it's versatile, and above all, it tastes great. Now it has become my standard for any recipe calling for bread dough; it works for Provençal fougasse and pissaladière as well as for just plain bread for sandwiches. Since I make this bread at least twice a week, I use a heavy-duty mixer to make it instead of kneading it by hand.

I did such a good job of teaching my friends how to make this bread that every time I travel to France, I have to bring an American heavy-duty mixer. I swap Kitchen Aid mixers for truffles, new recipes, etc., and everybody is happy.

Pâte à pain aux pommes de terre

Potato Bread Dough

THIS POTATO BREAD dough is a staple in my Provençal and New York kitchens.

In New York, I am lucky to have a very efficient and lovely housekeeper, Janina Tomczyk. As soon as Janina arrives in the kitchen, she chooses 3 medium baking potatoes (about 1¼ pounds), covers them with cold salted water, and cooks them. Making bread has become for her an automatic process. She stops briefly to add some flour in the heavy-duty mixer while continuing her many chores without losing a beat.

When making bread dough, remember that you can incorporate flour faster on humid summer days than on dry winter days; in winter, I stop adding flour after 2 cups (the dough might appear dry at this point) and wait 20 minutes before adding the other 2 cups of flour. Don't forget to peel and mash the potatoes as soon as they are cooked. Do not leave them in water, or let them get cold, or you'll have glue instead of mashed potatoes; wait for the mashed potatoes to cool before beating in the yeast mixture, or the yeast will be killed when it comes in contact with the heat. In winter, bread dough rises more slowly than in summer. If my kitchen is not very warm in the winter, I warm the bowl of the heavy-duty mixer before making bread and I turn on the electric oven to warm it up a bit. I turn the oven off 5 minutes later and place the dough in the oven to rise faster. You can keep the dough in the refrigerator for a week before baking it.

I always make 1 recipe of dough and cut off a quarter of it for an 8-inch pissaladière or half the dough for a fougasse. I keep the remaining dough in the refrigerator to make more pissaladières or I bake it for bread.

MAKES 2 POUNDS DOUGH

1¼ pounds baking potatoes (russet)

½ cup cold milk

1 tablespoon active dry yeast

1 teaspoon sugar

4 cups unbleached all-purpose flour

1 tablespoon salt

In a pan, cover the potatoes with cold salted water and bring to a boil. Partially cover and cook for 30 minutes or until tender.

Drain the potatoes, reserving ½ cup of potato water. Add the cold milk to the potato water. Sprinkle the yeast and sugar over it and set aside in a warm place for 15 minutes.

MAKING BREAD WITH A HEAVY-DUTY MIXER

Peel the *hot* potatoes and transfer them to the bowl of a heavy-duty mixer fitted with a flat paddle. Beat the potatoes until mashed. Wait for a few minutes until the potatoes are just warm.

Start beating the yeast mixture into the mashed potatoes. Mix the flour and salt together. Gradually beat in the flour, ¼ cup at a time at first. In winter, I stop adding flour after 2 cups. I wait 20 minutes before I continue adding the remaining flour. When the dough sticks to the beater and cleans the bowl, add the remaining flour tablespoon by tablespoon.

MAKING BREAD BY HAND

Mash the hot potatoes in a ricer in a large mixing bowl. Wait a few minutes for the potatoes to cool.

With a wooden spoon, stir the yeast mixture into the mashed potatoes. Mix the flour and salt together. Gradually beat in the flour, ¼ cup at a time; in winter, I stop adding flour after 2 cups. I wait 20 minutes before I continue adding the remaining flour. If the dough gets

Cover the bowl with a plastic bag.

Let rise at room temperature until the dough has doubled in size, about 2 hours in winter and 1 hour in summer.

Sprinkle flour on the risen dough and knead it for about 1 minute, adding more flour if necessary, especially during humid days, but remember the dough should be soft, much softer than for a classic bread dough. Refrigerate the dough covered with plastic wrap and follow the directions given in the recipes.

Baguettes

When I agreed to make hors d'oeuvres for 300 people attending a professional foodie event, I shaped my potato bread into baguettes. I baked the breads in my aging but never used baguette molds and they were perfect: easy to cut and well suited for the rillettes I spread on them.

If you have any leftovers, make croutons or toasts; I also reheat baguettes in the oven.

Makes four 16-inch-long and 2½-inch-thick baguettes

Potato Bread Dough (page 76), refrigerated after its first rising

1 teaspoon butter or olive oil, to grease the molds

1 tablespoon olive oil, to brush the top of the uncooked baguettes

Flour your hands and lightly knead the cold dough; it will be very soft.

Divide the dough in 4 pieces.

Brush butter or olive oil in baguette molds.

Shape each piece into a 16-inch-long sausage (the size of my baguette molds; adjust the length of the sausage according to your molds) and transfer the dough to the molds. The dough will only half-fill the molds at this point.

Clip the top every ½ inch with scissors. Brush olive oil over the top.

Heat the oven to 150 degrees (or warm) for 5 minutes. Turn off and place the bread molds in the turned-off oven for 30 minutes or until the dough fills the molds. Remove from the oven.

Preheat the oven to 400 degrees.

Bake in the middle of the oven for 20 minutes or until golden brown.

Unmold on a cake rack and wait ½ hour before serving.

Toasts

I MAKE small toasts with leftover baguettes.

1 16-inch-long baguette

3 to 4 tablespoons olive oil

Cut the baguette into ½-inch-thick slices.

Heat some of the olive oil in a nonstick skillet over medium heat. In batches, without crowding the skillet, add the bread slices. Cover the skillet and cook over medium heat for 3 minutes or until lightly golden, turning the bread once. Continue until all the bread is used.

I LIKE THE *fougasse aux olives* made by an innkeeper in Villeperdrix, a village clutching a hillside covered with olive groves near Nyons where my mother and my aunt were born.

Years ago my husband and I went there to fetch a birth certificate for my aunt, who lived in Arizona. She had written for it twice but had no answer at all from the *mairie* ("city hall") in Villeperdrix.

Villeperdrix is not easy to find; the village is hidden on the far side of a hill that is part of a small canyon and the turnoff is easy to miss. The Romans who had inhabited Provence called it Ville Perdue ("lost town"), but through the ages, the name changed to Ville Perdrix ("partridge town").

We arrived on a blazing hot, dry summer afternoon; the town was asleep but for one lonely goat that peeked at us through a barn door wondering what we were doing outside. Wandering through the empty streets for several minutes, I noticed a curtain moving ever so slightly. I knocked on the door to see a very old and very tiny lady:

"*Oui?*"

"*Bonjour, madame.* Can you tell me where I can find Monsieur le Maire?" (In France, as a sign of respect, *monsieur* or *madame* is always tacked on before the political title.)

"*Ah oui,* he is hoeing his potatoes."

"Where, *s'il vous plaît?*"

"*Par là-bas*" (a vague "over there").

We went *par là-bas* and indeed found the mayor hoeing his potatoes.

"*Bonjour, monsieur,* I am looking for Monsieur le Maire."

"*C'est ici.*" ("It's here.")

"We have come to fetch a birth certificate for Madame Dunn, who was born in Villeperdrix."

He looked at us and said in a most solemn voice: "*Ah, il y en a beaucoup qui se croient nés à Villeperdrix qui ne le sont pas!*" ("There are lots of people who think they were born in Villeperdrix, but they weren't!")

With my mouth hanging open, what could I say? I only knew I could not look at Wayne or I would have burst out laughing. Monsieur le Maire led us to the *mairie* and right away put his finger on the registration book in which my aunt's birth was registered. Triumphantly he said: "See, she was not born in Villeperdrix but in Léoux [the hamlet next door]!" From his tone of voice, I knew that people born in Villeperdrix were of a higher order than those born in Léoux!

He had not sent my aunt's birth certificate because she had not sent the price of a stamp to forward it.

I sometimes go to Villeperdrix these days to a small restaurant where the *fougasse aux olives* is good. Nowadays Villeperdrix is a large village with Danes, Belgians, and English who have bought summer houses there, but every time I go, I tell the story of the mayor who now is in heaven with his potatoes and his olives!

Fougasse aux olives

Olive Focaccia

A FOUGASSE IS a flat bread with open slits. It looks like a giant pretzel, but its closest relative is the Italian focaccia. You can bake it without any condiment kneaded into it or with anchovies, sardines, olives, tapenade, garlic, and herbs.

Pit the olives with a cherry pitter or a knife. Buy imported olives if possible. Niçoise or Gaeta olives are excellent.

One recipe of Potato Bread Dough will make 2 fougasses; if I make only 1 fougasse, I keep the other half of the dough in the refrigerator.

MAKES A 9 BY 14-INCH FOUGASSE

½ cup pitted Niçoise or
    Gaeta olives

½ recipe Potato Bread Dough
    (page 76), refrigerated
    after its first rising

1 tablespoon olive oil

Flour a pastry surface and knead the pitted black olives into the bread dough, poking the olives into the dough with your fingers as best you can.

On a floured pastry surface, gently roll the dough to a 9 by 14-inch oval and transfer it to an oiled nonstick jelly roll pan.

With large scissors, make eight to ten 4-inch slits in the dough and open them wide with your fingers.

continued

Brush olive oil over the top and cover with a large plastic bag to form a tent so the dough doesn't stick to the bag. Set aside and let rise until soft to the touch, about ½ hour in summer, 1 hour in winter. (The slits will have narrowed.)

Preheat the oven to 425 degrees.

Bake for 15 to 20 minutes or until the bottom and top of the bread are golden.

VARIATION

Fougasse à l'ail et au romarin

GARLIC AND ROSEMARY FOCACCIA

1 tablespoon minced fresh rosemary

1 tablespoon minced fresh garlic

Combine the rosemary and garlic and knead into the dough, before shaping it into a focaccia. Omit the olives.

Pissaladière aux aubergines

Eggplant Pissaladière

JAPANESE EGGPLANTS ARE the size of Provençal eggplants, 12 inches long and 3 inches in diameter. If they are unavailable, choose the smallest eggplants and cut the slices into wedges. If you prefer steaming the eggplants instead of deep frying them, see the note below.

MAKES ONE 8-INCH PISSALADIÈRE; SERVES 6

½ pound fresh mozzarella cheese, shredded (2 cups)

1 cup tightly packed shredded basil leaves

1 tablespoon minced garlic

1½ teaspoons salt

½ cup corn oil

Flour for dredging

1 pound eggplant, cut into ½-inch slices (about 4 cups)

¼ recipe Potato Bread Dough (page 76), refrigerated after its first rising

1 teaspoon olive oil

Combine the cheese, basil, garlic, and 1 teaspoon salt. Set aside.

In a large skillet, heat the corn oil over medium high heat. Dredge the eggplant slices or wedges in flour and shake off excess. Fry the eggplant until golden brown for 2 minutes. (Be sure the oil is hot before frying; otherwise the eggplant will retain too much oil.)

Drain the eggplant on paper towels and sprinkle with ½ teaspoon salt.

Preheat the oven to 450 degrees.

Roll the dough to a 13-inch circle on a floured pastry surface. Transfer the dough to an oiled nonstick jelly roll pan or cookie sheet. Spread the mozzarella mixture over the dough, leaving a 1-inch border.

Arrange the eggplant over the cheese. Fold the 1-inch edge over the filling. Brush the rims with olive oil.

Bake the pissaladière for 20 minutes or until the cheese is melted and the crust is golden brown.

continued

NOTE:

Instead of deep frying the eggplant slices, place them in a large lasagna pan. Dribble 1 tablespoon oil over them and pour about ¼ cup water in the pan. Cover with foil and bake for 30 minutes in a preheated 400-degree oven. Pat the eggplant slices dry with paper towels and proceed with the above recipe.

Pissaladière aux oignons

Provençal Onion Pissaladière

I AM LUCKY to have a husband who makes great salads with all the leftovers from my cooking classes, for which we invite good friends on the spur of the moment. I only need to make a fougasse, baguette, or this pissaladière for a perfect meal. If you don't like anchovies, just omit them, but don't reject this classic pissaladière.

MAKES A 10 BY 15-INCH PISSALADIÈRE

½ recipe Potato Bread Dough (page 76), refrigerated after its first rising

2 tablespoons olive oil

2 pounds onions, sliced (6 cups)

6 large garlic cloves, coarsely chopped

1 teaspoon salt

2 tablespoons minced fresh parsley

1 teaspoon fresh thyme leaves

6 to 8 anchovy fillets, packed in oil

Several Niçoise or Gaeta olives

Flour a pastry surface and rolling pin and roll the refrigerated dough to a 10 by 15-inch rectangle. Transfer it to an oiled nonstick jelly roll pan. Set aside until the dough is room temperature and soft, about 1 hour.

In a large nonstick skillet, heat 2 tablespoons olive oil over medium heat and add the onions and the garlic along with the salt, parsley, and thyme. Cook over low heat until lightly caramelized, adding more oil if necessary and occasionally stirring, about 10 to 20 minutes.

Preheat the oven to 425 degrees.

Drain the anchovies. Pat dry and slice each fillet into several thin julienne strips. Spread the onions over the dough.

Crisscross 2 anchovy strips all over the top of the onions and decorate with black olives.

Bake in the upper part of the oven for 20 minutes, until the onions and bread are lightly golden.

Serve warm.

Pissaladière aux poivrons rouges et aux tomates

Red Pepper and Tomato Pissaladière

I ALWAYS MAKE double the amount of peppers and tomatoes for this pissaladière so I have extra to serve with fresh pasta for another meal, and I've given those quantities if you want to do the same.

MAKES AN 8-INCH PISSALADIÈRE; SERVES 6

¼ recipe Potato Bread Dough (page 76), refrigerated after its first rising.

4 large red bell peppers

1 pound fresh tomatoes, peeled, seeded, and chopped (2 cups) (see Note, page 9)

4 large garlic cloves, minced

¼ cup olive oil

1 teaspoon salt

Freshly ground black pepper

2 cups freshly grated Gruyère cheese

¼ cup Niçoise or Gaeta olives

Preheat the oven to 425 degrees.

On a floured pastry surface, roll the dough to a 10-inch circle and transfer it to an oiled nonstick jelly roll pan. Cover it with a large plastic bag to form a tent so the dough doesn't stick to the bag, and let rise until the dough is puffy.

Char the peppers on top of the stove or barbecue them until they blacken completely. Place them in a sturdy plastic bag and set aside to cool.

Peel the peppers and remove the core and seeds. Cut them into 1-inch strips, then crosswise into 1-inch squares. You should have about 2 cups.

Combine the peppers and tomatoes in a mixing bowl and toss in the garlic, oil, salt, and freshly ground pepper. Toss and set aside.

Spread the grated cheese on top of the risen dough; scatter 2 cups of red pepper and tomato mixture over the cheese (refrigerate the remaining peppers and tomatoes for pasta; see below).

Scatter olives on top.

Bake for 20 to 30 minutes or until the bottom of the pissaladière is lightly golden. Serve warm.

VARIATION

Pâtes fraîches à la marmelade de poivrons et aux tomates

PASTA WITH RED PEPPER AND TOMATO RELISH

SERVES 2 OR 3

½ recipe Fresh Egg Pasta (page 31)   Gruyère, Parmesan, or goat cheese

2 cups cold red pepper and
    tomato mixture

Cook pasta until *al dente,* drain and toss in the cold red pepper and tomato mixture.

Grate Gruyère or Parmesan, or shred goat cheese over it. Toss and serve.

Pissaladière au fromage blanc et au lard fumé

Cheese and Bacon Pissaladière

MAKES ONE 8-INCH PISSALADIÈRE; SERVES 6

¼ recipe Potato Bread Dough (page 76), refrigerated after its first rising

8 ounces lean bacon, diced (1 cup)

¾ cup fresh farmer cheese or fresh goat cheese

¼ cup drained plain yogurt

4½ teaspoons minced garlic

½ cup basil leaves

½ teaspoon salt

2 medium tomatoes, cut into ¼-inch slices (2 cups)

1 teaspoon olive oil

Preheat the oven to 425 degrees.

On a floured pastry surface, roll out the dough to a 10-inch circle and transfer it to an oiled nonstick jelly roll pan. Cover with a large plastic bag to form a tent and let rise until the dough has puffed.

In a large nonstick skillet, brown the diced bacon. Drain on paper towels.

In the bowl of a food processor, combine the cheese, yogurt, garlic, basil, and ½ teaspoon salt and process until smooth.

Spread the cheese mixture on top of the risen dough and bury the bacon in the cheese. Cover the top with the tomato slices.

Bake for 20 to 30 minutes or until the bottom of the pissaladière is lightly golden brown.

Season with salt and drizzle olive oil on the pissaladière before serving. Serve hot or warm.

THE FOLLOWING pissaladières are tarts made with a short crust dough (*pâte brisée*). The Short Crust Dough, made with only unsalted butter, flour, and a very small amount of water, is in the dessert chapter, page 252. Eliminate the sugar in the dough for the savory tarts.

Tarte campagnarde à l'oignon

Country Onion Tart

JEAN LUC ABRAS, our flutist friend from Paris who loves to cook, makes this tart as soon as he arrives in Nyons to get him into the spirit of the region.

SERVES 6 TO 8

3 tablespoons olive oil	2 eggs
2 pounds onions, thinly sliced (6 cups)	1 tablespoon Dijon mustard
1 teaspoon salt	One 10-inch Partially Prebaked Tart Shell (page 253)
5 anchovy fillets, packed in oil	Several Niçoise or Gaeta olives

Preheat the oven to 425 degrees.

In a 6-quart dutch oven, combine the oil, onions, and salt with ¼ cup water. Cover and braise for 30 minutes, occasionally stirring the onions.

Pat dry the anchovy fillets with paper towels. Cut each anchovy fillet into julienne strips. Set aside.

Drain the onions. Set aside until cool. Combine the onions with the eggs.

Spread the mustard on the bottom of the prebaked tart shell and spread the onion mixture on top. Create a lattice pattern with the anchovy strips on top of the onions and add a Niçoise or a Gaeta olive in each diamond.

Bake in the middle of the oven until the top is golden brown, about 30 to 40 minutes.

Cut into wedges and serve at room temperature.

Tarte nyonsaise

Tomato, Cheese, and Olive Tart

DURING THE SUMMER I live in Nyons, dubbed the Petit Nice with a Promenade des Anglais and palm trees, just like the coastal Nice. According to the locals (including me), the best olives and the best olive oil come from Nyons. The olives are not plump but creased, with a very intense flavor, so intense that I find other varieties bland by comparison. In New York City, I occasionally find the Nyons olives, but they're not half as good as when I eat them in Nyons. I prefer Niçoise or Gaeta olives away from Nyons.

SERVES 6 TO 8

1 unbaked 10-inch Short Crust Dough tart shell, page 252

2 tablespoons Dijon mustard

1 egg

1½ cups freshly grated Gruyère cheese

About ten ¼-inch-thick tomato slices

Several Niçoise or Gaeta olives

1 teaspoon olive oil

Salt

Freshly ground black pepper

Preheat the oven to 425 degrees.

Whisk the mustard and egg together, then spread on the unbaked tart shell.

Sprinkle the cheese over the surface and decorate with the tomato slices, laying them flat on top of the cheese and leaving a small space between each slice. Add several olives. Dribble oil over the tomatoes.

Bake in the lower part of the oven for 30 minutes.

If the cheese is not golden brown, set the broiler on high and lightly brown the top of the tart for a few seconds.

Sprinkle salt and freshly ground pepper on the pissaladière and serve right away.

Tarte à la mozzarelle fumée

SMOKED MOZZARELLA TART

Substitute 1½ cups shredded smoked mozzarella for the Gruyère. But prebake the pastry (see A Partially Prebaked Tart Shell, page 253) before adding the mustard, egg, and cheeses; mozzarella, which is much wetter than Gruyère, will make the bottom of the tart soggy if it is not prebaked.

Tarte au soufflé de tomates et basilic

Tomato and Basil Soufflé in a Tart

ONE SUMMER I ate a delicious tomato and bread soup in the Cantinori Antonioni in Florence. I could not wait to go back to Nyons, my Provençal home, to experiment with it. I loved the taste but not the presentation (thick soups have never appealed to me). First, I decided to make it into individual light soufflés using just egg whites, no yolks, baked in a water bath. I served them unmolded around a roasted leg of lamb. Finally, I realized I needed an easier presentation. While I was testing recipes for this chapter, I had a brainstorm in my sleep. Why not cook the soufflé in a prebaked tart shell? We had *Tarte au soufflé de tomates et basilic* for lunch that day. It was a hit! The gossamer texture of the filling is a perfect contrast to the rich pastry.

SERVES 6 TO 8

4 tablespoons olive oil

1 large onion, thinly sliced (2 cups)

6 garlic cloves, minced

2½ pounds fresh tomatoes, peeled and coarsely chopped (5 cups) (see Note, page 9) or two 35-ounce cans Italian plum tomatoes, chopped and drained (save the juice for a soup)

1 teaspoon sugar

1 teaspoon salt (less if you use canned tomatoes)

¼ cup fresh basil leaves

Pinch of cayenne

1 cup crustless bread cubes

2 egg whites

One 10-inch Partially Prebaked Tart Shell (page 253)

In a large skillet, heat the oil over medium heat. Stir in the onion and garlic and cook for 5 minutes, stirring often to avoid burning the garlic.

Add the tomatoes, sugar, salt, basil, and cayenne. Cover and cook for 15 minutes. Uncover and mash the bread into the tomatoes with a fork until thoroughly mixed. Cook until the tomatoes have the consistency of a thick relish, about 15 minutes, depending on how watery the tomatoes are. Taste and add more salt if necessary. Preheat the oven to 400 degrees.

Beat the egg whites until firm. Fold the egg whites into the tomato mixture and pour into the prebaked tart shell.

Bake for 20 to 25 minutes or until the top is lightly golden.

Serve hot or at room temperature, cut into 6 or 8 wedges.

VARIATION

Petits soufflés de tomates

INDIVIDUAL TOMATO SOUFFLÉS

FOR A DINNER party, I still make this soufflé in individual molds.

Preheat the oven to 400 degrees. Oil ten ½-cup ramekins or baba molds. Fill the molds with the tomato–egg white mixture and place in a water bath. Bake for ½ hour or until the top is golden brown.

Unmold the soufflés around a roasted leg of lamb or other roast.

Tourte de courgettes provençales

Zucchini Cobbler, Provençal Style

PROVENÇAL GRANDMOTHERS, just like grandmothers everywhere in France, kept their handwritten recipes in old calendar-agendas during the first half of this century. I have collected several grandmothers' agendas, which I treasure. This recipe comes from the agenda of Maurice Pinard's grandmother. I spent an afternoon listening to his enthusiastic telling of Provençal lore and Provençal cooking, which he learned from his grandmother. Monsieur Pinard graciously gave me this recipe. I cherish it, in part because I have never seen anything comparable.

Make 2 recipes of Short Crust Dough (*Pâte brisée*), one for a prebaked tart shell and the second one to roll out for the top of the cobbler.

MAKES 12 SMALL SERVINGS

1 pound small zucchini, cut into ¼-inch cubes (4 cups)

2 teaspoons salt

2 tablespoons olive oil

2 medium leeks, tough green leaves discarded, chopped (2 cups)

2 garlic cloves, minced

2 eggs

⅓ cup grated Parmesan cheese

Freshly ground black pepper

One 10-inch Partially Prebaked Tart Shell (page 253)

Short Crust Dough (page 252)

FOR THE EGG GLAZE

1 egg mixed with 1 teaspoon water

Place the zucchini cubes in a colander and sprinkle with 1 teaspoon salt. Set aside for 30 minutes.

In a large nonstick skillet, heat the olive oil over low to medium heat. Add the leeks and cover.

Braise for 10 minutes, stirring occasionally. Leeks, like onions, burn easily; if they do start to burn, quickly add ¼ cup water.

Rinse the zucchini cubes under cold water and pat dry with paper towels.

In a large mixing bowl, combine the raw zucchini, the cooled braised leeks, garlic, eggs, Parmesan cheese, and season with the remaining salt and freshly ground pepper.

Preheat the oven to 400 degrees.

Fill the prebaked shell with the zucchini-leek stuffing.

On a floured pastry surface, roll out the short crust dough to a 13-inch circle.

Cover the zucchini tart with the circle of dough and trim the edges. Reserve the pastry trimmings to make decorations for the top of the cobbler or for another small tart.

Cut small incisions in the pastry cover to let steam escape during baking.

Brush the glaze over the top.

Bake for ½ hour to 15 minutes or until golden on top.

Eat warm.

Fish

WE ARE SO FAR inland in Nyons that we eat fish only on market day, Thursday. I am up at dawn to beat the lines that form early in front of my fishmonger and to avoid being exasperated by the activities of the linebusters—a bunch of old ladies (I know them all) who arrive last and end up first on line. There are three fishmongers in the Nyons market, but we, the Nyonsais, go to the one on the Place des Arcades because we think he has the freshest fish. My husband has bought very good fish from the others. He buys his *friture* (little fish, fried whole, heads and all), knowing we will fight over which fish we'll eat that day: his *friture* or whatever fish I fancied.

My fish repertoire is small because of taste and geography. Most Thursdays, however, in Nyons, I prepare fish either for lunch or for dinner.

On Bouillabaisse

IN JUNE AND September, when I teach cooking in Nyons, market day is bouillabaisse day. I order the fish a week ahead to be sure the ones I need will not be sold out before I get there. Sometimes, the fishmonger disappoints because of bad weather. The rock fishes (galinettes, rascasses, St. Pierre, etc.) required for an authentic bouillabaisse are unavailable because of rough seas. I have to make substitutions, just as I do when I am in New York.

A bouillabaisse is a whole meal in Provence and served only on special occasions. My fishmonger in Nyons is thrilled when he sees me and always includes an extra fish, on the house, in my shopping bag.

After buying the fish with my students, we split up to explore the market. We gather back at the house by 11:00 A.M. and start cooking. I have already gutted and cleaned the fish, pricking my fingers with all those sharp scales, muttering to myself that I'll never make a bouillabaisse again. But by 1:00 P.M., we are all set to serve the bouillabaisse on the terrace, where we enjoy the sun and a great meal washed down with several bottles of local Chardonnay. Soon, I eagerly anticipate next week's bouillabaisse, even the fish cleaning.

Bouillabaisse, New York Style

A BOUILLABAISSE IS a whole meal; I like to serve the fish broth first with croutons and rouille or aioli. Next comes the fish itself with steamed or boiled potatoes, more broth and rouille or aioli. I follow it with a tossed green salad and a simple dessert.

In New York, what fish should I buy? Even more important, what fish should I buy for the broth? Years ago, I could find small butterfish or whitings; today I never see them. Cod, halibut, and snappers are too expensive and too fragile to cook just for the broth, yet the flavors and subtlety of the broth are the most important part of a bouillabaisse. Nowadays, I buy fish from Seku, who oversees the excellent fish department at Dean & DeLuca. I call him a day or two before making the bouillabaisse to reserve heads of red snapper, halibut, or other heads and bones from white-fleshed fish (though none from oily fish). If you can get a monkfish head (retail stores usually receive big fish without their heads) take it, for the broth will be that much better. In Nyons, only once have I been able to buy monkfish head—it is the most prized for a bouillabaisse broth.

Most important, the fish heads must be very fresh, gills removed. If the heads are very big, have them cut up. For anyone allergic to shellfish, add 1 more pound of fish heads to the broth and eliminate the mussels in this recipe.

Monkfish is the fish I like to poach in the broth and eat as a second course. Fortunately, monkfish is widely available in the States. I order it in advance and ask the fishmonger to cut and fillet a 4-pound chunk, reserving the central bone for the broth.

A bouillabaisse should be shared with friends in the making as well as in the eating.

SERVES 6

4 pounds monkfish, filleted

5 pounds fish heads and
monkfish bones

3 tablespoons Pernod

1 teaspoon saffron threads or more

½ cup olive oil

2 onions, coarsely chopped
(about 2 cups)

4 large garlic cloves, chopped

2 cups chopped fennel bulb

2 ½ pounds fresh tomatoes,
chopped (5 cups), or two
28–ounce cans Italian plum
tomatoes, chopped and
drained (save the juice
for a soup)

1 tablespoon minced fennel leaves

1 tablespoon salt or more

1 tablespoon fennel seeds

1 bay leaf

3 sprigs of fresh thyme

1 strip of dried orange peel

3 pounds fingerling potatoes

2 pounds mussels

Rouille (recipe follows) or Aioli
(page 104)

Cut the monkfish into 6 pieces. Chop the bone and reserve it for the soup.

On a large platter, rub the monkfish, the monkfish bone, and the fish heads with Pernod and half of the saffron threads.

In one large pot (I use my 9-quart dutch oven), heat the olive oil over medium heat. Cook the onions, garlic, and fennel bulb for 5 minutes, stirring occasionally.

Add the tomatoes and the fennel leaves; sprinkle with 1 teaspoon salt and cook for 10 minutes.

Add the fish heads and the monkfish bone to the tomatoes. Sprinkle with 2 teaspoons salt and cook for 5 minutes, prodding the fish with a wooden spatula to break it up into smaller pieces.

Bring 4 cups water to a boil.

Add the fennel seeds, the last of the saffron, the bay leaf, thyme, and orange peel to the dutch oven. Pour in the boiling water, bring to a rolling boil. Continue cooking over high heat for 20 minutes.

Strain the soup through a fine-meshed strainer, pushing on the fish with the back of a large spoon to extract all the flavors; discard the fish debris. You should have 5 cups of fish broth.

Bring the broth back to a boil. Poach the monkfish over medium high heat, turning the fish over in the broth for 15 minutes. After 10 minutes, I cut into a piece of monkfish to see how much longer it will take to cook. The fish must be cooked through.

Meanwhile, in a large pan, cover the potatoes with salted cold water and cook until tender, about 20 minutes.

Transfer the fish to a preheated platter and set aside.

Add the mussels to the broth. Cover and bring to a boil over high heat. As soon as the mussels open, transfer them to a bowl. Strain the soup through cheesecloth to remove any sand that may have clung to the mussels.

Taste the broth and add more salt if necessary and reheat it.

Serve the broth first with half the mussels, croutons, and 1 batch of rouille or aioli.

Next, serve the fish, more mussels with the potatoes, and more rouille or aioli.

Rouille

Makes 1¹/₂ cups

½ cup crustless bread cubes

3 large garlic cloves, minced

1 egg yolk

¼ teaspoon powdered saffron

3 tablespoons bouillabaisse broth
    (page 100)

½ teaspoon salt

¹/₁₆ teaspoon cayenne or more

½ cup olive oil

½ cup corn oil

In the bowl of a heavy-duty mixer, combine the bread, garlic, egg yolk, saffron, fish soup, salt, and cayenne.

At medium speed, beat the mixture until smooth. Drop by drop, whisk in the oils; it takes about 10 minutes. If the mixture still looks lumpy, dribble in more broth.

Taste and correct seasoning with salt and cayenne if necessary. For more information on mounting a mayonnaise, see the instructions for Aioli (page 104).

Grand Aioli

I PLAY HOSTESS on most summer Thursdays. In the morning, friends come to shop at the market in Nyons and end up around my table for lunch. Grand Aioli lends itself to a large number of guests; it's a dish of poached salted cod with a spread of boiled or steamed vegetables all slathered in aioli, the Provençal garlic mayonnaise. And if by noon, the number of unexpected guests exceeds the amount of food in the house, Wayne quickly goes to the market (it's at the foot of the château) to buy spit-roasted chickens to add to the grand aioli. Add any vegetable you wish to the ones listed below and a cold roasted chicken. It's an easy dish but not an impromptu one because you must soak the salt cod for at least 12 hours.

SERVES 8

2 pounds salt cod

2 red bell peppers

2 yellow bell peppers

1½ teaspoons salt

Freshly ground black pepper

2 pounds boiling potatoes (fingerlings)

1½ cups Chardonnay

½ pound tender green beans, ends snapped

1 large cauliflower

½ cup Niçoise or Gaeta olives

Aioli (recipe follows)

Put the salt cod in a large bowl of cold water in the sink under a trickling of running water for 1 to 2 hours. Keep refrigerated overnight in cold water. Drain the salt cod.

In a medium saucepan cover the cod with cold water. Bring to a near boil and poach for 20 minutes in the quivering water. Drain and set aside.

Char the peppers on top of the stove. Wrap them in a plastic bag. Set aside to cool.

Peel the peppers and cut them into large strips. Season with ½ teaspoon salt and freshly ground pepper. Set aside.

In a pan, cover the potatoes with cold salted water. Bring to a boil and cook until tender. Peel them while they are hot and toss them in the wine with ½ teaspoon salt and freshly ground pepper.

continued

In a large saucepan, bring several quarts of salted water to a boil. Add the green beans and boil until just cooked through but still crisp, 3 to 4 minutes. Drain and season with the remaining salt and freshly ground pepper. Set aside.

Bring several quarts of salted water to a boil in a large saucepan.

Break the cauliflower into florets; discard the large stem of the cauliflower or reserve for a soup.

Plunge the florets in the boiling water. Boil for 5 minutes. Drain.

Decoratively place the vegetables on one platter, the poached salt cod with black olives on another, and the aioli in a bowl.

Aioli

TO MAKE AIOLI, I mix equal parts olive oil with corn oil to balance the overwhelming fragrance of the olive oil.

During wintertime, warm the bowls, whisks, and eggs before making the aioli; the warmth will help thicken it.

MAKES 1 CUP

6 large garlic cloves	Pinch of cayenne
Pinch plus ½ teaspoon salt	½ cup olive oil
2 egg yolks, at room temperature	½ cup corn oil

Peel the garlic cloves, split in two, and remove and discard the germ, if any. Chop coarsely and add to the bowl of a food processor. Add a pinch of salt and process for 1 minute.

In the bowl of a heavy-duty mixer, combine the egg yolks, garlic, salt, and cayenne.

At high speed, slowly dribble ⅛ teaspoon of oil at a time into the egg yolks, increasing it to ¼ teaspoon when the mixture thickens.

At this point, the aioli will be very thick. Add 1 tablespoon water and beat just enough to smooth the aioli. Refrigerate for up to 24 hours. Bring to room temperature before serving.

Taste and correct seasoning.

If the aioli does not thicken, or if it curdles, transfer it to a small bowl. Wash and dry the aioli bowl and whisk.

Break 1 egg yolk into the cleaned bowl and whisk or beat in the curdled aioli, *drop by drop,* into the yolk. It will start thickening; beat or whisk in the remaining oil (if there is any left) of the curdled aioli.

Two reasons for failed aioli: cold weather and putting the oil in too fast. Warm up bowls and whisks. Warm up the eggs and oil in hot water. Dribble the oil in very, very slowly.

Crevettes assaisonnées à l'estragon

Shrimp in a Tarragon Dressing

I SERVE THIS shrimp dish with Old-Fashioned Mashed Potatoes (page 222).

SERVES 6

¼ cup olive oil

3 pounds large shrimp, shelled and deveined; shells reserved

1 large fresh tomato, chopped

⅔ cup Chardonnay

1½ teaspoons salt or more

1 cup heavy cream

1 tablespoon minced fresh tarragon

Freshly ground black pepper

In a large nonstick skillet, heat half the oil over medium high heat. Sauté the shrimp shells for 1 minute. Add the tomato, wine, ½ teaspoon salt, and ½ cup water and bring to a boil. Reduce the heat and simmer for 10 minutes.

Add the cream and the tarragon and simmer for several minutes longer.

Strain the cream sauce into a saucepan, pressing hard on the shells; discard the shells. Reduce the sauce over high heat to about ⅔ cup.

In the same nonstick skillet, heat the remaining 2 tablespoons oil. In 3 batches, with ⅓ teaspoon salt per batch, sauté the shrimp for 5 minutes or until cooked through.

Combine the shrimp and the cream sauce; sprinkle with freshly ground pepper. Taste and correct seasoning.

Serve on a bed of mashed potatoes.

Ragoût de lotte aux champignons sauvages

Stew of Monkfish and Wild Mushrooms

IN THE FALL in Nyons I cook monkfish with *cèpes* or chanterelles. In New York, I substitute shiitake or portobello mushrooms if wild mushrooms are not available.

SERVES 4

½ pound *cèpes*, chanterelles, shiitake, or portobello mushrooms

1 teaspoon coarsely cracked black pepper

1 teaspoon salt

1 pound monkfish fillets, patted dry

¼ cup olive oil

1 large garlic clove, minced

1 tablespoon minced parsley

2 tablespoons minced shallots

½ cup Chardonnay

4 tablespoons unsalted butter, cut into pieces

Clean the mushrooms with damp paper towels. Discard the tough stems and cut the caps in ½-inch wedges.

Combine the pepper and ½ teaspoon salt on a large plate. Roll the monkfish fillets in the mixture.

In a large nonstick skillet, heat 1 tablespoon oil over medium heat. Add the mushrooms, garlic, parsley, and remaining ½ teaspoon salt. Cover, lower the heat, and braise for 10 minutes.

In a large nonstick skillet, heat the remaining oil over high heat. Sauté the monkfish on all sides for 4 to 5 minutes. Cover, and over medium heat, braise for about 5 minutes. Transfer the fillets to a cutting board. Slice the fish crosswise into ½-inch medallions.

Add the shallots and wine to the mushrooms. Over high heat deglaze the pan, scraping the bottom of the pan with a wooden spoon for 1 minute. Remove the skillet from the heat and whisk in the butter, piece by piece.

Toss the fish in the mushroom-butter sauce. Taste and correct seasoning. Serve immediately.

Filet de saumon grillé

Broiled Salmon Fillet

MY AUNT, WHO was also my adopted mother, was born in Villeperdrix, near Nyons. Tatane created this simple way of broiling salmon fillet. She heated the broiler pan, then placed the salmon fillet skin side up in the pan. The underside cooks immediately upon contact with the very hot pan; by the time the top is broiled the skin is charred and the fillet is cooked just so, without drying.

This method yields very moist salmon with an appealing charred skin.

Serve the salmon with White Bean Stew (page 253), Old-Fashioned Mashed Potatoes (page 222), or Fresh Egg Pasta (page 31).

SERVES 4

2 pounds salmon fillet   **Salt**

Lemon wedges

Set the broiler on high for 10 minutes.

Set the oven rack 5 inches away from the heating element. Place an oiled broiler pan or a cast-iron skillet on the rack and heat for 10 minutes.

Place the fish, skin side up, on the hot pan or skillet.

Broil the fish for 10 minutes or until the skin is charred.

Serve as is with lemon wedges and salt on the side.

Poisson en papillote à la menthe et au pastis

Fish Steaks in Papillote with Mint and Pernod

IN NEW YORK, I make this with salmon, halibut, or tuna steaks. I serve the fish with Fresh Egg Pasta (page 31) or Old-Fashioned Mashed Potatoes (page 222).

SERVES 4

1 tablespoon olive oil

4 fish steaks, 1 inch thick (10 to 12 ounces each)

3 tablespoons Pernod or Ricard

¼ cup shredded fresh mint

1 teaspoon salt

Freshly ground white pepper

Line a large baking dish with a generous amount of parchment paper to overhang the side of the dish. Drizzle the oil over the paper.

Place the steaks in the dish and sprinkle them with Pernod and mint. Season with salt and freshly ground white pepper.

Enclose the fish in the paper by bringing the sides of the paper over the fish, folding and crimping to seal. Set aside for 2 hours. (If you refrigerate the steaks, bring them back to room temperature before baking.)

Preheat the oven to 400 degrees.

Bake the fish in the middle of the oven for 20 minutes.

Unwrap the fish and transfer it to a preheated platter. Serve the papillote juices in a sauceboat.

Poisson poché

Poached Codfish

ON THURSDAYS in Nyons, I broil, bake, or poach fish. For poaching, I buy a thick slice of *colin* or lieu noir. In New York, I poach cod.

SERVES 6 TO 8

5 pounds cod (in 1 thick slice, about 5 inches wide, 8 inches long)

1 onion, quartered

3 sprigs of parsley

2 large garlic cloves, unpeeled

1 tablespoon salt

½ dozen black peppercorns

½ cup basil leaves

2 pounds fingerling potatoes

Several salad leaves, washed and spun dry

Niçoise or Gaeta olives (for garnish)

Tomato wedges (for garnish)

Lemon wedges (for garnish)

Aioli (page 104) and/or Brandade (see below)

In a large heavy-bottomed pan, cover the fish with cold water. Add the onion, parsley, garlic, salt, and peppercorns.

Bring the water to a boil on medium high heat. It should take about 40 minutes for the water to come to a boil. When the boil is reached, turn off the heat, add the basil leaves, tightly cover the pan, and set aside for 15 minutes.

Meanwhile, steam the fingerling potatoes for 20 minutes.

Transfer the fish to a large plate. Set aside for 15 minutes. Skin and bone the fish. Decorate a large platter with salad leaves. Put the fish in the center of the platter with the steamed potatoes around it. Decorate with olives, wedges of tomatoes, and lemons. Serve the aioli or the brandade on the side.

Brandade

THE FIRST TIME you taste brandade, a salt cod mayonnaise, it will be love or hate at first bite. I love it with raw or steamed vegetables, with steamed or mashed potatoes, and with cold chicken. But when I serve it, I make sure to have an aioli on the table with it; the brandade is for me, the aioli is for Wayne.

MAKES 2 CUPS

8 ounces salt cod	$\frac{2}{3}$ cup heated olive oil
2 garlic cloves, peeled and coarsely chopped	$\frac{1}{2}$ cup boiling milk
	$\frac{1}{4}$ cup heated heavy cream

Put the salt cod in a large bowl of cold water in the sink under trickling running water for 1 to 2 hours. Keep refrigerated overnight in cold water. Drain the salt cod.

In a medium saucepan cover the cod with cold water. Bring to a near-boil and poach for 20 minutes in quivering water. Drain.

In a food processor, process the cod and garlic for 1 minute. With the motor running, drizzle the hot oil and milk alternately through the feed tube, scraping down the work bowl as necessary.

Reheat the brandade over low heat and gradually stir in the hot cream.

Set aside to cool. Taste and correct seasoning.

Friture

Small Fried Fish

MY HUSBAND'S FAVORITE Thursday lunch in Nyons is a *friture*. He buys tiny fish with heads and all. Served fried with a tossed green salad and washed down with a cold crisp white or rosé wine, I also eat them with gusto. In New York, I buy white-baits or any small silvery fish the size of an anchovy.

SERVES 4

2 pounds tiny fish	Flour for dredging
1 quart corn oil	Salt

Wash the fish under running cold water. Pat dry with paper towels.

In a large deep fryer or a wok, heat the oil to 325 degrees.

Just before frying, dredge the fish in flour and shake off excess. Fry until golden brown, about 4 to 5 minutes. Do the dredging and the frying in batches.

Sprinkle the fish with salt and serve immediately.

Soupe de moules safranées

Mussel Soup in a Saffroned Sauce

WHEN MUSSELS ARE fresh, they retain their liquor, but as they age they lose it. In Nyons, 4 pounds of steamed mussels yield 5 cups of mussel broth; in New York, I get about 2 cups. Supplement the mussel broth with chicken or fish broth if necessary.

To clean mussels, brush them with a small wire brush. Be sure they are closed. Throw out heavy mussels, which are generally full of sand.

SERVES 8 FOR A FIRST COURSE; 4 FOR A MAIN DISH

4 pounds mussels, scrubbed
    and cleaned

2 tablespoons minced shallots

1 cup Chardonnay

Light Broth (page 11)

4 tablespoons olive oil

4 tablespoons flour

¼ cup heavy cream

⅛ teaspoon ground saffron

1 tablespoon freshly squeezed
    lemon juice

2 tablespoons minced garlic

Salt, if necessary

Toasts (page 79)

In a large kettle, combine the mussels, shallots, and wine. Cover and steam over high heat, shaking the pan occasionally, until the mussels open. With a wire-mesh strainer, transfer the mussels to a large bowl as they open.

Discard the shells, reserving the mussels. Strain the mussel broth through cheesecloth to remove any sand. Measure the broth; add Light Broth (page 11) or mussel broth to make 5 cups.

In a large saucepan, heat olive oil. Stir in flour, whisking until smooth. Add the broth, cream, saffron, lemon juice, and garlic. Simmer over medium heat, partially covered, for 30 minutes, whisking from time to time.

Taste and add salt if necessary.

Reheat the mussels in the sauce.

Serve in deep bowls with toasts and a chilled Chardonnay.

Un turban de rizoto aux fruits de mer

Molded Risotto with Shellfish

CLOVISSES, THE TINY CLAMS of Provence, are described in the *Larousse Gastronomique* as "not only remarkable for their beauty, but known for their cleanliness. They live on only the finest sand, avoiding mud and hating any kind of pollution." In the States, the New Zealand cockles are just as clean, but if you can't find them, substitute small clams.

The dish is worth all the work it involves; the presentation is beautiful and its taste is excellent. I make it for special occasions.

SERVES 8

1 pound small shrimp

2 pounds mussels

2 pounds cockles or small clams

2 tablespoons olive oil

1 tablespoon flour

2 teaspoons freshly squeezed
    lemon juice

4 tablespoons tomato sauce
    (page 8 or page 10)

2 cups round starchy rice such
    as Arborio

FOR THE SHRIMP SAUCE

2 tablespoons olive oil

Reserved shrimp shells

1 tomato, quartered

1 cup Chardonnay

$^1/_2$ cup heavy cream

1 sprig of thyme

In saucepan, boil 1 quart water. Add the shrimp and boil 5 minutes. Drain the shrimp, reserving the liquid for the risotto.

Peel and devein the shrimp; reserve the shells for the shrimp sauce.

In a large pot, combine the mussels and cockles with $^1/_2$ cup water. Cover and bring to a boil. As soon as the shellfish open, transfer them to a bowl.

Discard mussel and cockle shells, saving a few for garnish.

Line a strainer with cheesecloth and filter the mussel and cockle broth, and reserve.

In a medium saucepan, heat 1 tablespoon oil and whisk in the flour until smooth. Add 1 cup of the filtered mussel and cockle broth, the lemon juice, and the tomato sauce. Cook over medium heat for 3 minutes. Add the mussels, cockles, and shrimp. Cover and set aside.

Prepare the risotto. Rinse the rice under cold running water. Drain. In a large nonstick skillet, heat 1 tablespoon olive oil and sauté the rice for 1 minute. Add the reserved shrimp broth and the remaining mussel and cockle broth, cover tightly, and cook very slowly for 20 minutes, or until the rice is tender.

While the risotto cooks, prepare the shrimp sauce.

In a large nonstick skillet, heat the oil over high heat. Sauté the shrimp shells and the tomato for 3 minutes.

Add the wine, cream, and sprig of thyme. Cover and cook over low to medium heat for 20 minutes.

Strain the sauce, pushing on the shells and tomatoes to extract the liquid. Set aside.

For an elegant presentation, fill an oiled, preheated 4-cup ring mold with the risotto. Tap the mold on the counter to be sure the rice is well packed; unmold on a preheated serving platter.

Reheat the shellfish and fill the center of the risotto mold with it. Decorate the sides with the reserved mussel and cockle shells.

For a simpler presentation, place the reheated shellfish in the center of a platter and surround with the rice.

Reheat the shrimp sauce and serve it in a sauceboat.

Daube de thon à la provençale

Provençal Tuna Stew

TUNA IS A difficult fish to cook properly. It requires juggling the oven's temperature. When the tuna is perfectly cooked, not dry, it is very good; even slightly overdone, it's good. Every time I make this dish, I shuffle between very good and good!

SERVES 4

2 red bell peppers

2 pounds tuna steak

2 anchovy fillets, mashed

2 tablespoons olive oil

1 onion, chopped (1 cup)

2 garlic cloves, minced

2 pounds fresh tomatoes, peeled, seeded, and chopped (4 cups)

½ cup basil leaves

½ teaspoon salt

Freshly ground black pepper

1 tablespoon capers

1 pound mussels, scrubbed and cleaned

½ cup Chardonnay

Char the peppers on top of the stove. Place in plastic bag and set aside to cool. Peel, core, and chop the peppers. Reserve the pepper juices. Set aside.

With the blade of a knife, make incisions in the fish and in them bury the mashed anchovy.

In a 6-quart dutch oven, heat the oil. Add the onion and garlic and cook for 5 minutes, stirring occasionally.

Add the tomatoes, basil, ½ teaspoon salt, and freshly ground pepper. Cover and simmer over medium heat for 15 minutes.

Preheat the oven to 325 degrees.

Place the fish steak on top of the tomatoes. Cover and bake in the oven for 15 minutes.

Add the peppers, pepper juices, and capers. Lower the oven temperature to 250 degrees and bake for 15 more minutes with the cover on.

In a large pot, add the mussels and wine. Cover and bring to a boil over high heat. With a wire mesh ladle, transfer the opened mussels to a bowl.

Strain the mussel broth through a strainer lined with cheesecloth.

Add the mussels to the fish. Serve with the mussel broth in a sauceboat.

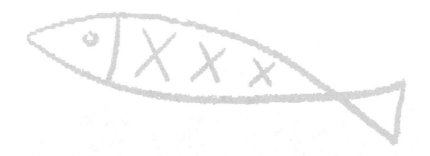

POULTRY AND GAME

Chicken

Poulet rôti flambé au pastis • 122
   (Chicken Flambéed with Pastis)

Coquelets à la provençale • 124
   (Provençal Cornish Game Hens)

Poulet au yaourt et à la moutarde • 125
   (Chicken with Yogurt and Mustard)

Fricassée de poulet aux citrons confits • 126
   (Chicken Fricassee with Preserved Lemons)

Ailerons de poulet en gigots • 128
   (Gigots of Chicken Wings)

Guinea Hens

Pintade rôtie à la drômoise • 130
   (Roasted Guinea Hen from the Drôme)

Pintades grillées au citron • 131
   (Broiled Guinea Hens in Lemon Juice)

Quail

Cailles braisées aux légumes sur un lit de couscous • 133
   (Braised Quail with Vegetables Served with Couscous)

Squabs

Pigeons rôtis aux échalotes • 135
  (Roasted Squabs with Shallots)

Rabbits

Lapin à la sarriette et au coulis de tomates • 137
  (Rabbit with Fresh Savory in a Tomato Sauce)

Fricassée de lapin à l'aioli • 138
  (Fricassee of Rabbit with Aioli)

Pheasants

Faisans rôtis au gros sel • 140
  (Roasted Pheasants in Kosher Salt)

Wild Boar

Daube de marcassin • 144
  (Wild Boar Stew)

Since the sixteenth century, when Henri IV decreed that every French household should have a chicken cooking in a pot every Sunday, chickens have been a symbol of prosperity in France. For many of my friends and neighbors in the South of France who are not farmers, a "farm" chicken is still a prize, and they are sure to mention to you how difficult it is to find a farmer who will raise "free range" chickens, in other words, real chickens.

For many years, I cooked a *coq au vin* for my husband's birthday in August, and every year I would ask the farmer to reserve a rooster for the following year and every year the rooster came, fortunately with feathers plucked, weighing around 3½ pounds. I used a cleaver to chop this muscular bird into pieces. After several hours of cooking, the sauce was full of rich flavors, and the bird was tender and yet chewy. The *coq au vin* birthday celebration on August 14 became so popular that I always ended up with a very small portion, generally with the comb of the rooster! The farmer was seduced by modernization and there are no more roosters for Wayne on his birthday.

In the southern part of the Drôme hills, farmers raise guinea hens, a cross between a chicken and a pheasant. They are much appreciated in our part of the country. In the States, if you are able to buy one, be sure it has not been frozen, for it will be tough and dry, as will rabbits. These fowl do not benefit from freezing. All the recipes in this chapter can be made with chicken if you wish.

Poulet rôti flambé au pastis

Chicken Flambéed with Pastis

PASTIS, A LICORICE DRINK, is to Provence what the mint julep is to Kentucky. You can't go to the south of France and not drink a pastis, it's just not done; plus you'll endear yourself to the locals if you try it. Marcel Pagnol in his trilogy, *Marius, Fanny,* and *César,* made pastis the drink of drinks. There are two famous commercial names, Pernod and Ricard, plus the thousands of homemade pastis.

Good accompaniments are Roasted Fennel (page 207) or Fondue of Fennel (page 208).

SERVES 4

One 3-pound free-range chicken

1 teaspoon salt

Freshly ground black pepper

1 branch of fennel, cut into
  $\frac{1}{2}$-inch-thick slices ($\frac{1}{2}$ cup)

1 tablespoon olive oil

1 carrot, cut into $\frac{1}{4}$-inch slices
  ($\frac{1}{2}$ cup)

1 medium onion, chopped (1 cup)

1 garlic clove, unpeeled

1 sprig of fresh thyme

2 tablespoons Pernod or Ricard pastis

Preheat the oven to 400 degrees.

Trim all the fat from the chicken cavity and neck. Cut off the wing tips and the second joints. Sprinkle $\frac{1}{2}$ teaspoon salt and freshly ground pepper in the cavity of the chicken and add the fennel. Truss the chicken and rub it all over with olive oil.

Place the chicken breast side down in a roasting pan.

Chop the wing tips and second joints and scatter them around the chicken with the carrot, onion, garlic, and thyme. Pour $\frac{1}{2}$ cup water over the vegetables and sprinkle with the remaining salt.

Roast the chicken, breast side down, for 40 minutes, basting occasionally and adding more water when necessary.

Turn the chicken breast side up, and roast for 40 minutes or until golden brown, basting and adding more water when needed.

Transfer the chicken to a cutting board with grooves and set aside for 10 minutes.

To flambé the chicken: With a gas burner, heat the pastis in a ladle. Tip the ladle toward the gas flame to ignite. Pour over the chicken (don't panic when the chicken is surrounded by flames, they will subside quickly). With an electric burner, heat the pastis in a small pan. Strike a match and ignite the pastis. Pour over the chicken.

Carve the chicken in serving pieces and pour the juices that spew out into the roasting pan. Discard the chicken wings in the pan and degrease the juices. Reheat and serve with the vegetables in a sauceboat.

Coquelets à la provençale

Provençal Cornish Game Hens

SERVE THIS WITH rice or Mashed Potatoes with Goat Cheese (page 221).

SERVES 4

2 Cornish hens

1 cup flour

1 tablespoon fresh thyme leaves

1½ teaspoons salt

Freshly ground black pepper

2 tablespoons olive oil

2 onions, thinly sliced (2 cups)

1 large garlic clove, minced

1 pound fresh tomatoes, peeled, seeded, and chopped (2 cups) (see Note, page 9) or one 14-ounce can Italian plum tomatoes, drained (save the juice for a soup)

¼ cup fresh basil leaves

½ teaspoon sugar

Cut off the wing tips and second joint of the wings. Reserve for a chicken broth. Split the Cornish hens in half lengthwise alongside the breast bone. Remove the back bone (again reserving it for a chicken broth) and carve each half into 4 serving pieces: two half breasts with the first joint of the wing attached, and two legs with thighs attached.

Combine flour, thyme leaves, 1 teaspoon salt, and pepper in a bowl.

Heat olive oil in a large nonstick skillet over medium high heat. Dredge a few pieces of fowl at a time in the prepared flour, shaking off the excess.

Brown the fowl for 10 minutes, turning the pieces over to color on all sides. Transfer to a plate and set aside. Repeat with the next batch.

Stir the onions and garlic into the same skillet, and cook until onions are wilted. Add the tomatoes and basil; sprinkle with the remaining salt, pepper, and sugar. Cook over medium heat for 5 minutes.

Place the Cornish hens on top of the tomatoes. Cover and cook over medium heat for 30 minutes. To serve, transfer the hens to a cutting board and halve them. Place the tomatoes on a platter and top with the hens. Serve immediately.

Poulet au yaourt et à la moutarde

Chicken with Yogurt and Mustard

THIS IS THE easiest recipe I know. My French neighbor Yvette Lebourge prepares the chicken in the morning before going to work and whoever in the family arrives home first in the evening puts the chicken in the oven. She makes more than she needs so they have leftovers, which she serves cold the next evening with a tossed green salad.

SERVES 8

1½ cups plain yogurt

⅓ cup strong Dijon mustard

½ teaspoon salt

Freshly ground black pepper

1 teaspoon fresh thyme leaves

2- to 3-pound free-range chicken, trimmed of all fat and cut into 8 parts each or 4 pounds chicken parts, trimmed of all fat

In two 2-quart baking dishes, mix the yogurt and mustard. Season with salt, pepper, and thyme.

Dunk the chicken parts in the mixture. If prepared several hours ahead, cover the pans.

Preheat the oven to 400 degrees.

Bake the chicken uncovered in the middle of the oven for 45 minutes or until golden brown.

Transfer the chicken parts to a serving platter.

Process the curdled yogurt sauce in the food processor or blender to smooth out the sauce and pour in a sauceboat. Serve immediately with Fresh Egg Pasta (page 31).

Fricassée de poulet aux citrons confits

Chicken Fricassee with Preserved Lemons

THIS MIDI VERSION of a popular Moroccan dish comes from a friend's mother, Triscilla Basiaux, who learned to make it years ago in Arles.

Preserved lemons can be bought in specialty stores or you can make your own (page 14). Serve the fricassee on a bed of Mashed Potatoes with Goat Cheese (page 221).

SERVES 6

Two 2½-pound free-range chickens

2 tablespoons olive oil

2 medium onions, thinly sliced (2 cups)

2 large garlic cloves, thinly sliced

2 cups 1-Hour Rich Broth (page 12)

⅛ teaspoon ground saffron strands

½ teaspoon salt

Freshly ground black pepper

1 Preserved Lemon (page 14), cut into 6 wedges

1 small sprig of rosemary

Cut off the wing tips and the second wing joints from the chickens; reserve for a chicken broth. Cut each chicken into 6 serving pieces: 2 thighs, 2 legs, and 2 boneless breast halves, each with the first joint of the wing attached. Trim the fat from all the pieces.

In a large nonstick skillet, heat the oil over medium high heat. Add the chicken breasts, skin side down. Brown the breasts, turning them over once, until golden brown (3 minutes on each side). Set aside on a plate.

Brown the thighs and legs, turning them occasionally (about 10 minutes). Set aside with the breasts.

Discard most of the fat in the skillet. Add the onions and garlic and cook, stirring occasionally, for 3 minutes.

Pour in the broth and sprinkle with the saffron. Bring to a boil and boil 2 minutes. Transfer the chicken back to the skillet, skin side up. Season with salt and freshly ground pepper.

Discard the pulp of the preserved lemon. Split the lemon rind in half lengthwise. Scatter the lemon strips on top of the chicken pieces. Add the rosemary sprig. Cover and simmer for 20 minutes.

Transfer the chicken and lemon strips to a preheated platter. Discard the rosemary.

Boil the cooking juices down to 1 cup. Pour the sauce over the chicken and serve immediately.

Ailerons de poulet en gigots

Gigots of Chicken Wings

THESE CHICKEN WINGS are trussed into small legs (gigots), to make presentation attractive enough for a dinner party.

The wings can be shaped the day before (a tedious process until you get the hang of it), and the sauce can be made ahead of time, too. The day of the party, you just need to sauté the wings.

The wings are excellent without the sauce, and the sauce is excellent with other chicken recipes. I suggest serving the chicken with White Bean Puree (page 243), Green Pea Puree with Garlic (page 210), or Old-Fashioned Mashed Potatoes (page 222).

SERVES 4

24 chicken wings

FOR THE SAUCE
2 tablespoons olive oil

Second joints and wing tips

1 cup diced celery root

2 carrots, cut into ¼-inch slices (1 cup)

1 onion, thinly sliced (1 cup)

1 fresh tomato, quartered

2 sprigs of fresh rosemary

4 cups Light Broth (page 11)

2 tablespoons olive oil

1 teaspoon salt

2 tablespoons lemon juice

2 tablespoons minced garlic

Paper frills

Cut off the wing tip and the second joint of each wing and reserve for the sauce. The first joint (where the wing meets the body of the chicken) is shaped into small gigots (legs).

To shape the gigots, with your left hand wrapped in a towel, take hold of one end of the joint. With a knife in your right hand, cut off the sinews and push the skin and meat toward the far end of the joint, making a small bundle with most of the bone exposed. It should look like a small Popsicle. This step can be done 24 hours ahead of time. Keep well wrapped in the refrigerator.

To make the sauce, heat 2 tablespoons olive oil in a large nonstick skillet, and brown the second joints and the wing tips until golden brown.

Add the vegetables and sauté for 5 minutes, stirring once in a while.

Add the rosemary and 2 cups light broth. Bring to a boil and simmer until reduced by half.

Pour in the remaining broth and continue simmering until you have about 1½ cups liquid left. Strain, pushing on the vegetables to extract as much liquid as possible (can be done up to 24 hours ahead of time). Set aside.

In a large nonstick pan, heat 2 tablespoons olive oil over medium heat. Brown the wings evenly on all sides (about 20 minutes). Season with salt. Transfer the chicken pieces to a platter.

Add the reserved sauce, lemon juice, and garlic in the skillet and boil down until lightly syrupy. Taste and correct seasoning.

Slip a paper frill on the exposed bone of each wing. Place 6 wings on each plate and serve the sauce in a sauceboat.

Pintade rôtie à la drômoise

Roasted Guinea Hen from the Drôme

MANY IN THE Drôme prefer guinea hens to chickens because the *pintades de la Drôme* are bred on farms there and are as famous as the *poulets de Bresse*. They are roasted in the simplest way; with tomatoes, onion, and fresh rosemary sprigs. Substitute chicken if guinea hen is unavailable. The roasted guinea hen can be served with Peas Braised with Salad Greens (page 209).

SERVES 4

One 2½-pound guinea hen

1 teaspoon salt

Freshly ground black pepper

1 tablespoon olive oil

2 sprigs of rosemary

2 fresh tomatoes, cut into eighths

1 onion, quartered

Preheat the oven to 425 degrees.

Trim all the fat from the hen's cavity and neck. Cut off the wing tips and second joints and chop into pieces. Set aside.

Sprinkle the cavity with ½ teaspoon salt and freshly ground pepper.

Oil a roasting pan large enough to fit the hen and the vegetables. Place the hen in the pan, breast side down, and tuck rosemary sprigs under the wings.

Scatter the reserved wing tips and second joints, tomatoes, onions, and the remaining salt around the bird. Pour ½ cup water over the vegetables.

Place the roasting pan on the middle shelf of the oven and roast for 1¼ to 1½ hours, turning the hen breast side up after 30 minutes (roast for 1 hour if you substitute chicken). Baste occasionally and add more water when necessary.

Let the hen rest for 10 minutes before carving into 4 servings. Pass the sauce in a sauceboat.

Pintades grillées au citron

Broiled Guinea Hens in Lemon Juice

SUBSTITUTE CHICKENS if guinea hens are unavailable. In the summer, Wayne grills the birds on our American grill and in the winter, I broil them in the oven. I suggest serving them with Eggplant Gratin from the Vaucluse (page 200).

SERVES 8

¼ cup lemon juice

3 tablespoons cold-pressed olive oil

1 tablespoon minced garlic

1 teaspoon salt

1 sprig of fresh rosemary

Three 2½-pound guinea hens, each cut into 6 parts

Combine the lemon juice, oil, garlic, salt, and rosemary in a bowl.

Preheat the broiler for 10 minutes before broiling.

Arrange the hen pieces skin side up on a rack set over a broiler pan.

Broil, basting occasionally with the lemon juice, until golden brown (about 15 minutes). Turn the pieces over and broil another 10 minutes, basting occasionally.

Transfer the breast pieces, skin side up, to a serving platter and continue broiling the legs and thighs for 5 minutes more.

Transfer them to the serving platter.

Remove the rack and pour the juices from the broiler pan into a small saucepan with the leftover lemon juice baste, if any, and reheat.

VARIATION

Barbecued Guinea Hens

IN THE SUMMER, our entertaining is informal and casual. With a glass or two of white wine in hand, we chat and drink around the barbecue.

To make grilling easier, disjoint the hens and cut into 8 parts: wings, boned breast pieces, legs, thighs.

continued

Prepare a good deep bed of coals, about 5 inches from the grill rack if possible. Keep a water squirter on hand for flare-ups.

First grill the legs and thighs, skin side down, and after 10 minutes, put on the wings. It will take about 20 to 30 minutes total cooking time, depending on your grill and fire.

Watch the grill all the time to take care of flare-ups and to keep the hen pieces from burning. Occasionally, brush some lemon juice baste on the top sides of the pieces. Turn 2 to 3 times during broiling to make sure they cook evenly.

When about 10 minutes remain, put the breasts on and watch closely to be sure they don't burn.

Test a piece or two near the end of cooking by making an incision with a sharp-pointed knife. The meat near the bone should still be juicy, but not pink.

Remove pieces to a platter and while still hot brush them all over with the remaining lemon juice.

It can keep for an hour, the time to eat the first course.

Cailles braisées aux légumes sur un lit de couscous

Braised Quail with Vegetables Served with Couscous

PETER BLOM, my Danish neighbor in Nyons, was inspired by all the produce in our weekly market to make poached quail. Poached in a very tasty broth with vegetables, saffron, and butter, they were the best quail I had ever eaten.

This dish can be prepared in two stages. First, I make the broth 1 or 2 days ahead; the day of the dinner, I poach the quail.

The taste of this dish is subtle but the way to eat quail is not. I use my fingers and have finger bowls for everyone.

SERVES 6

Steamed Couscous (see below)

6 quail

3 cups 1-Hour Rich Broth
(page 12)

1 carrot, peeled and cut into
$\frac{1}{8}$-inch-thick slices
($\frac{1}{2}$ cup)

1 small white of leek, cut into
juliennes ($\frac{1}{2}$ cup)

1 large shallot, peeled and
quartered ($\frac{1}{4}$ cup)

3 medium garlic cloves, quartered
($\frac{1}{8}$ cup)

$\frac{1}{4}$ teaspoon saffron threads

$\frac{1}{2}$ teaspoon salt

3 tablespoons unsalted butter, cut up

Watercress or mâche (for garnish)

Set aside prepared couscous.

Place the quail in 1 large sauté pan that fits them comfortably. Cover with the broth and add the vegetables, saffron, salt, and butter.

Bring the broth to a boil, lower the heat to a high simmer, and cover the pan. Poach at a high simmer for 40 minutes, turning the birds over once in a while in the broth.

I serve each quail nested in couscous, with some poaching vegetables on and around the quail; I ladle broth around, not on, the couscous. The remaining broth is served in a sauceboat. Decorate with clusters of watercress or mâche.

continued

Couscous à la vapeur

STEAMED COUSCOUS

IN NEW YORK, I buy loose couscous, which I prefer to the packaged precooked couscous. I always cook a large amount of couscous so I can use leftovers to make a couscous salad mixed with grapefruit, corn, peas, and tomatoes and tossed in a vinaigrette dressing.

1 cup golden raisins	6 tablespoons olive oil
½ cup 1-Hour Rich Broth (page 12) or water	Several saffron strands
½ teaspoon salt	4 cups medium-grain couscous

Soak the raisins in the broth for 30 minutes.

In a medium saucepan, combine 1 cup water, salt, oil, and saffron. Bring to a boil.

Spread the couscous and the raisins in a jelly roll pan and pour the boiling water on the couscous. Stir the couscous with a fork until all of it is wet. Set aside 30 minutes.

Bring 3 quarts water to a boil in a couscoussier or a stockpot. Line the steamer part of the couscoussier or a fine-mesh strainer with a double thickness of cheesecloth.

Rub the couscous in your hands to get rid of lumps. Transfer it to the lined steamer or strainer. Cover and steam over medium heat for 30 minutes.

Fluff the couscous with 2 forks before serving it.

Pigeons rôtis aux échalotes

Roasted Squabs with Shallots

I AM VERY lucky to have Gustave Tortel as a friend. He lives high in the hills of St. Dizier where he cultivates potatoes and lavender for his living, and raises pigeons and beehives for his pleasure. I am so spoiled, I hope I don't become like the gourmet guru of *L'il Abner* who was dying of starvation at age 99 because nothing was good enough for him. Gustave is doing this to me—after eating his pigeons, it is difficult to eat commercial squabs. And his honey! Just imagine bees fluttering on the lavender and bringing it back home to concoct honey. I love it and I don't even like honey!

I'm forced back to earth when I return to New York. Substitute Cornish hens if you prefer them to squabs.

I like to serve them with Cornmeal Galettes with Raisins (page 240); I place a galette in the center of each plate with a squab piece on top and ladle the sauce and shallots over the squabs.

SERVES 4

Four 1½-pound squabs

4 small sprigs of rosemary

2 tablespoons olive oil

12 large shallots, peeled

1½ cups 1-Hour Rich Broth (page 12)

1 teaspoon salt

Freshly ground black pepper

Preheat the oven to 450 degrees.

Remove the wing tips and second joint and reserve for a broth.

Place a sprig of rosemary in the cavity of each bird.

Arrange the squabs, breast side up, in a shallow roasting pan or a gratin dish. Dribble the oil over the squabs. Scatter the shallots around the birds and pour in ½ cup broth. Sprinkle with salt and freshly ground pepper.

Roast the squabs for 15 minutes. Pour the remaining 1 cup of broth into the pan and roast the birds for 10 to 15 minutes longer, basting occasionally, until golden brown. (Roast Cornish hens 45 minutes and baste with more broth.)

Transfer the birds to a platter.

continued

Carve each bird into 4 parts: 2 legs with thighs attached and 2 half breasts with the first joint of the wing attached.

Pour the juices that spewed out during the carving of the birds back into the roasting pan and reheat.

NOTE:

You can prepare the whole dish in the afternoon and reheat it as follows: Place the pigeons on a broiler pan. Cover and set aside. Heat the broiler just before serving and place the birds 5 inches from the heat and broil to crisp the skin. Reheat the sauce.

Lapin à la sarriette et au coulis de tomates

Rabbit with Fresh Savory in a Tomato Sauce

I HAVE A friend in Buis-les-Baronnies who raises rabbits and sells them in local weekly markets. She often makes this simple dish with *sarriette* (savory), an herb similar to thyme. Serve it with Fresh Egg Pasta (page 31).

SERVES 4 TO 6

6 tablespoons olive oil

One 2½-pound rabbit (a fryer), cut into 10 parts

2 medium onions, sliced (2 cups)

2 large garlic cloves, coarsely chopped

1 teaspoon salt

Freshly ground black pepper

½ cup Chardonnay

2 cups tomato sauce (page 8 or 10)

3 sprigs fresh savory or thyme

½ pound white onions, peeled

½ pound small shiitake mushrooms, stems discarded

In a large nonstick skillet, heat 2 tablespoons oil. When the oil is very hot, brown half of the rabbit pieces for 5 minutes, turning occasionally.

Stir in half the sliced onions and garlic and brown for 5 more minutes. Watch carefully, making sure not to burn the onions and garlic. Transfer the rabbit pieces and onions to a 6-quart dutch oven. Season with ½ teaspoon salt and freshly ground pepper.

Repeat with the second batch of rabbit.

Pour the wine in the skillet and bring to a boil, scraping the bottom of the skillet to get up the drippings. Add the tomato sauce to the wine and mix.

Pour the wine-tomato mixture over the rabbit and toss. Add 2 sprigs of savory or thyme. Cover and cook over medium heat for 1½ hours or until tender, occasionally turning the rabbit over.

Heat the remaining 2 tablespoons olive oil in a pan. Add the white onions and the mushroom caps. Season with salt and pepper, and add a sprig of savory or thyme.

Cover tightly and braise for 15 minutes.

Reheat the rabbit with the white onions and mushrooms. Serve hot with the pasta.

Fricassée de lapin à l'aioli

Fricassee of Rabbit with Aioli

SERVES 4 TO 6

One 2½-pound rabbit (a fryer),
    cut into 10 parts

FOR THE MARINADE

10 large garlic cloves, peeled

2 sprigs of fresh thyme

1 sprig of fresh rosemary

½ teaspoon salt

Freshly ground black pepper

1 tablespoon olive oil

1 cup robust red Côtes du
    Rhône or zinfandel

FOR COOKING THE RABBIT

½ cup olive oil

1 pound fresh tomatoes, peeled,
    seeded, and chopped (2 cups)
    (see Note, page 9)

1 cup Light Broth (page 11)

½ teaspoon salt

Freshly ground black pepper

Aioli (page 104)

In a large bowl, combine the rabbit with the garlic cloves, herbs, salt, freshly ground pepper, oil, and wine. Toss the rabbit in the mixture. Cover and marinate overnight in the least cold part of the refrigerator.

Drain the rabbit pieces and reserve the marinade.

Pat dry the rabbit and the garlic cloves with paper towels.

In a large skillet, heat the oil. When very hot, fry the rabbit pieces in batches (do not overcrowd the pan), turning occasionally until golden brown, about 15 minutes.

Transfer the rabbit to a plate. Sauté the garlic cloves until lightly golden. Transfer to a plate.

Sauté the tomatoes for 2 minutes. Set aside with the rabbit. Discard most of the fat in the skillet, leaving 1 tablespoon.

Return rabbit, garlic, and tomatoes back into the skillet. Pour the marinade and light broth over the rabbit. Sprinkle with salt and freshly ground pepper. Cover and simmer for 1 to 1½ hours, occasionally turning over the rabbit pieces in the sauce.

Transfer the rabbit and garlic to a serving dish. Strain and degrease the sauce. Serve as is or with an aioli and steamed potatoes.

Faisans rôtis au gros sel

❧

Roasted Pheasants in Kosher Salt

ROASTING PHEASANT IN a salt crust guarantees a moist flesh, which is not always the case with conventional roasting. Years ago, at the home of friends in the town of Die in the Drôme, I ate a pheasant baked in a salt crust. It was moist and tender but my hostess had a terrible time discarding the salt; the crust had disintegrated and stuck to the bird. Joel Robuchon, the French chef of chefs, devised a salt crust that's easier to discard.

As soon as the pheasants are wrapped in the salt crust, bake in the oven.

Cabbage Chartreuse (page 197) is a good choice to accompany the pheasants.

SERVES 8

SALT CRUST FOR EACH PHEASANT

2 cups coarse salt (I use
    kosher salt)

1 tablespoon fresh thyme leaves

1 tablespoon rosemary needles

2 egg whites

2$\frac{1}{2}$ cups all-purpose flour

Two 2$\frac{1}{2}$-pound female pheasants

Sauce Poivrade (opposite) and/or
    Cranberry Sauce (page 145)

Prepare the crust at least 2 hours or up to 24 hours before roasting the fowl. In a large bowl, combine salt, herbs, egg whites, and $\frac{2}{3}$ cup water. Gradually beat in the flour and knead until firm. If the dough is too sticky, add more flour. Cover with plastic wrap and set aside.

Cut off the wing tips and the second joints of the pheasants and reserve for the sauce poivrade.

Discard clusters of fat from the cavities and with paper towels, wipe the pheasants dry.

Flour a pastry surface and carefully roll out the salt dough (it has the tendency to break up) large enough to enclose the fowl.

Preheat the oven to 500 degrees.

Put the salt-wrapped fowl in an oiled roasting pan and roast in the very hot oven for 45 minutes.

Remove the pheasants from the oven and set them aside for 30 minutes before discarding the salt crust.

Cut the pheasant breasts parallel to the breast bone into ¼-inch slices. Carve the legs with the thighs attached.

Serve with Sauce Poivrade and/or Cranberry Sauce.

Sauce Poivrade

SAUCE POIVRADE IS a classic. Though it involves many steps, it can be prepared a day or two before the dinner.

Make sauce poivrade in three stages: First, prepare the light broth. Second, make a rich sauce with meat, vegetables, wine, and light broth. Third, finish the poivrade sauce with a caramel-vinegar base. The 2 cups of rich broth from the second stage will be enough for 2 batches of the caramel-vinegar base. I urge you to make 2 batches of caramel-vinegar base; if you double the base, the poivrade sauce will be too sweet; sometimes doubling amounts in recipes will not work.

MAKES 2 CUPS SAUCE; SERVES 8

FOR RICH SAUCE (2 CUPS)

1 bottle robust red wine
(zinfandel, Côtes du Rhône)

1 tablespoon vinegar

2 tablespoons vegetable oil

2 pounds veal breast or beef
stew meat

2 medium onions, chopped
(2 cups)

2 carrots, cut into ¼-inch
slices (2 cups)

1 cup chopped celery root

1 celery branch, cut into ¼-inch slices
(1 cup)

1 teaspoon crushed black peppercorns

10 juniper berries

½ teaspoon salt

1 quart Light Broth (page 11)

continued

Caramel-Vinegar Base

(FOR EACH 1 CUP RICH SAUCE)

2 tablespoons sugar

3 tablespoons water

1 tablespoon vinegar

1 cup rich sauce

2 tablespoons butter

In a large pan, bring the wine to a boil. Strike a match and flambé the wine. Shake the pan until the flame subsides, about 3 minutes. Add the vinegar and set aside.

In a large pan, heat the oil over medium heat. Brown the meat, turning the pieces over until evenly browned.

Add the vegetables and brown for 5 minutes.

Add the crushed peppercorns and juniper berries, and sprinkle with the salt. Pour the wine and the Light Broth over the meat and vegetables.

Cook over medium heat for 1½ hours, occasionally skimming and discarding the fat and scum on the surface.

Remove the meat and reserve for sandwiches or salad. Strain the sauce through a fine-meshed sieve into a pan. Reduce the sauce to 2 cups, if necessary.

For the caramel-vinegar base, combine the sugar and water in a saucepan. Bring to a boil and cook until the syrup thickens and colors to amber. Turn off the heat. Quickly add the vinegar and 1 cup rich sauce.

Whisk in the butter and whisk continuously until the sauce is the perfect consistency, lightly thickened and with a shiny gloss.

Repeat with another batch of caramel-vinegar base and the remaining 1 cup rich stock.

Wayne and the Visiting Wild Boars

YEARS AGO IN our cottage in the hills, I heard strange noises in my sleep. Finally I realized I was not dreaming, the noises were pig grunts. I woke up Wayne; not impressed with my tale of wild boars, he turned around and went back to sleep.

Several years later while picking *girolles* (chanterelles) with our neighbor Bébert, Wayne noticed that the ground had been torn up and the bark was rubbed off the trees, "It's the boars who play, scratching themselves against trees while hunting for mushrooms just like us," said Bébert. Not known to lose an advantage, I said, "See, Wayne, I was right, there are boars here." He remained unconvinced.

On a very peaceful and lazy afternoon, Wayne had his comeuppance and I had my revenge. Wayne was cleaning the car trunk when I heard him yell; I rushed outside to see my husband staring at very large papa and mama boars, no more than 5 feet away. Boars, Wayne, and I stood still for what seemed forever until the boars made the first move. After having looked Wayne over, they passed him and continued their afternoon stroll. That time I kept my mouth shut . . . until now.

In the fall, during hunting season, every farm kitchen anticipates making stews of wild boars. Whoever shoots a boar will split it among the villagers. Stews are prepared ahead of time and eaten several days later. In New York, I use venison.

Daube de marcassin

Wild Boar Stew

TRADITIONALLY, THE STEW is served with polenta. I like Cornmeal Soufflé (page 238) or I prepare Gnocchi with Morels (page 242). If you cannot find boar or venison, substitute shoulder of pork.

SERVES 6

4 pounds wild boar or venison, cut into 1½-inch cubes

2 carrots, cut into ½-inch slices (1 cup)

1 medium onion, quartered

1 celery branch, cut into ½-inch slices

4 garlic cloves, mashed

2 sprigs of fresh thyme

3 cups robust red wine, Côtes du Rhône or zinfandel

1 tablespoon red wine vinegar

3 tablespoons olive oil

2 teaspoons salt

Freshly ground black pepper

Flour for dredging

1 to 2 cups Light Broth (page 11) or water

Cranberry Sauce (see below)

In a large bowl, combine the meat, vegetables, and thyme. Pour in the wine, vinegar, and 1 tablespoon olive oil. Sprinkle with 1 teaspoon salt and freshly ground pepper. Toss together the meat, vegetables, and seasoning.

Cover the bowl and marinate in the least cold part of the refrigerator for 2 days, tossing occasionally.

Drain the meat and vegetables in a large colander, reserving the marinade.

Preheat the oven to 300 degrees.

Pat the meat dry with paper towels.

In a large nonstick skillet, heat 2 tablespoons oil over medium high heat. Dredge the meat with flour, shake off excess. Brown the meat in several batches to avoid overcrowding the skillet, which will create steamed meat. It will take about 20 minutes to brown the meat. Transfer the meat to a 9-quart dutch oven.

Brown the vegetables in the same skillet for 5 minutes and add to the meat.

Pour the reserved marinade in the skillet and bring it to a boil. Pour over the meat and vegetables and add enough broth or water to barely cover the meat.

Cover the dutch oven tightly and bake in the middle shelf of the oven for 3 hours. Discard the fat on top of the sauce.

Serve the Cranberry Sauce on the side.

Sauce aux Airelles

CRANBERRY SAUCE

MAKES 2 CUPS

1 cup sugar   2 cups fresh cranberries

1 cup water

Combine the sugar and water in a saucepan and bring to a boil. Boil 5 minutes to thicken the syrup. Add the cranberries and simmer uncovered over low to medium heat without stirring for 5 minutes.

Pour into a sauceboat.

BEEF AND VEAL

Beef

Daube dioise • 149
    (Winter Beef Daube from Die)

Boeuf aux carottes • 151
    (Braised Beef with Carrots)

Gardiane de boeuf • 152
    (Beef Stew from the Camargue)

Boeuf en casserole des mariniers du Rhône • 154
    (Beef Shanks Braised in Onions from the Bargemen
    of the Rhone)

Raviolis niçoises • 156
    (Ravioli from Nice)

Pot au feu du Midi • 158
    (Boiled Dinner from the South)

Veal

On Veal Breast • 160

Tendrons de veau poêle à la dioise • 160
    (Veal Breast Spareribs with Fresh Tomatoes)

Tendrons de veau grillés • 162
    (Grilled Veal Spareribs with Lemon and Fresh Mint)

Blanquette de veau du Midi • 163
    (Veal Stew from the South)

Jarrets de veau en cocotte aux petits oignons • 164
    (Veal Shanks Braised with Pearl Onions and Tarragon)

AT THE TABLES of my friends in northern Provence, meat is served after the vegetable course. Still seen as a luxury, meat is expensive and only small quantities are served to be savored and appreciated. I feel cheated though when I don't have meat and vegetables served together, and sometimes I even ask my hostess to serve them that way. She looks surprised, but after all what do you expect from a New Yorker!

During twenty-five summers spent in the South of France—either in the hills of the Diois region or in the town of Nyons—I have never had a dinner in friends' homes where meat was served rare. It is traditional to braise or roast meat for a long time. Meat and fowl are braised in black iron dutch ovens on top of the stove, making the basting easy, while the vegetables cook slowly in the oven.

Today many of my friends have modern stoves, fueled with butane gas, on which they cook during the hot summer days; but in cooler weather, their homes are still heated with wood stoves on which they cook. That's the best time to be invited for dinner: the smells are so good—it would convert a vegetarian. Nothing is comparable to the aroma and warmth of a kitchen enrobed in the fragrance of a wood fire or to raising the lid of the dutch oven and inhaling the explosion of scents. I am so satisfied by the smells that I think I eat less when the food is served.

Meats slowly braised will render a lot of pan juices, which are used to flavor the vegetable gratins served later in the week or to make Ravioli from Nice (page 156).

IN NEW YORK as in the Midi, I buy beef shanks for braising; it's a perfect cut, not at all stringy. A shank weighs between 7 and 8 pounds with the bone. Boned, beef shanks are called shin of beef. There is a large muscle running through the meat that can be removed when the meat is boned for stews; I do not bother to remove it when I cook the shank with its marrow bone for the Boiled Dinner from the South (page 158).

Daube dioise

Winter Beef Daube from Die

IN FRANCE, I have two butchers: Monsieur Gonnet in Luc-en-Diois near our small cottage in the hills and Monsieur Dinnelle in Nyons, where we now spend most of the summer. Lucienne Gonnet is my source for simple, succulent dishes. She works alongside her husband, day in and day out, and hasn't much time to spend in the kitchen, but when she does, she prepares for several meals.

She calls this recipe a daube *provençale*, but it is very different from the traditional daube I know. The meat is poached in water with vegetables, then cooked in a tomato sauce with olives from Nyons.

Ask the butcher to bone the beef shank (keep the bone for stock) and remove the large muscle that runs through the shank.

Make the daube at least 2 to 3 days before you need it; it ages well.

As a suggestion, serve the daube with Old-Fashioned Mashed Potatoes (page 222), Semolina Gnocchi with Morels (page 242), or Cornmeal Soufflé with Mushrooms (page 239).

SERVES 6

4 pounds boned beef shank
  (shin of beef), fat trimmed
  and meat cut into 1½-inch-
  thick cubes

1 onion, stuck with 2 cloves

1 cup ½-inch-thick slices carrots

½ cup ½-inch-thick slices
  celery branch

A bouquet garni (a large bouquet
  of parsley tied with several
  sprigs of thyme or 1 teaspoon
  dry thyme wrapped in cheesecloth and a bay leaf)

2½ teaspoons salt

One 28-ounce can Italian plum
  tomatoes, drained and chopped
  (save the juice)

2 tablespoons olive oil

1 cup chopped onion

1 tablespoon minced garlic

2 tablespoons flour

1 strip of dried orange peel

continued

Place the meat and 8 cups cold water in a 9-quart dutch oven. Bring to a boil; skim and discard the scum that rises. (It will look very unappetizing, but the tomato sauce will fix everything.)

Add the vegetables and bouquet garni, and sprinkle with 2 teaspoons salt.

Partially cover and simmer on medium high heat for 1½ hours.

With a large skimmer, transfer the meat and the vegetables to a bowl and set aside. Discard the bouquet garni and the onion. Strain the broth, reserving the vegetables.

Preheat the oven to 300 degrees.

Boil down the tomato juice saved from the can until it thickens and reduces to 1 cup.

In the washed dutch oven, heat the oil over medium heat. Add the chopped onions and garlic. Cook for 5 minutes, stirring occasionally.

Sprinkle with the flour and stir for 1 minute.

Add the tomatoes, the reserved vegetables (carrots and celery from the broth), the orange peel, the tomato juice, and 3 cups broth. Cover and simmer for 30 minutes.

Add the meat, cover and braise the daube in the middle of the oven for 1½ hours, stirring occasionally. If the sauce thickens too much, add more broth.

Boeuf aux carottes

Braised Beef with Carrots

I REMEMBER MY mother making *Boeuf aux carottes* when our farmer friends could bring us beef and carrots during World War II; it was her favorite beef stew.

To bring out the flavor of the carrots, make the stew a day or two ahead and reheat very slowly. In New York, I generally prefer packaged carrots from the supermarket rather than buying bunches of carrots from gourmet stores; the former have more flavor.

Remove the muscle that runs through the beef shank before cutting it in cubes.

SERVES 6

4 pounds boned beef shank (shin of beef), fat trimmed and cut into 1½-inch cubes

2 medium onions, thinly sliced (2 cups)

3 large garlic cloves, minced

4 tablespoons olive oil

3 sprigs of thyme or 1 teaspoon dry thyme tied in cheesecloth

2 teaspoons salt

Freshly ground black pepper

2 pounds carrots, peeled and cut into ¼-inch slices (5 cups)

Divide the meat, onions, and garlic into 2 batches.

In a large nonstick skillet, heat 2 tablespoons oil over medium high heat. Sauté, stirring meat, onions, and garlic for 4 to 5 minutes, adjusting the heat to avoid burning the onions and garlic. Remove meat from skillet and repeat steps for second batch.

Transfer the meat and onions to a 9-quart dutch oven. Add the thyme and sprinkle with 1 teaspoon salt and freshly ground pepper. Pour in 1½ cups water and cover tightly. Braise over a low simmer for 2 hours. The cooking juices should quiver slightly at all times; be sure the lid is on tight and if steam escapes, lower the heat even more.

In a mixing bowl, toss the carrots with 1 teaspoon salt. Stir them into the meat and onions. Cover tightly and, over a low simmer, braise for 45 minutes or until the carrots are tender.

Reheat the next day.

Gardiane de boeuf

Beef Stew from the Camargue

A *gardiane* is a beef stew from the Camargue (French cowboy country), north-west of Marseilles. Elizabeth David raves about this simple Provençal dish in *An Omelette and a Glass of Wine*: "the Gardiane brought tears to our eyes; we had been overwrought and dropping with fatigue, and while the food we had already eaten had cheered and comforted us, it wasn't until the cover was taken off the dish of beef stew and we smelt the wine and the garlic and the rich juices and saw the little black olives and the branches of wild thyme which had scented the stew laid in a little net-work over the meat, that the tension vanished. . . ."

In the fall, I serve the *gardiane* with Pumpkin Gratin (page 223).

SERVES 6

3 tablespoons olive oil

4 pounds boned beef shank
(shin of beef), fat and muscle
discarded, cut into
2-inch pieces

¼ pound small white onions,
peeled (1 cup)

¼ pound mushrooms,
quartered (1 cup)

6 whole garlic cloves, peeled

½ cup tomato sauce (page 8 or
page 10)

1 cup dry white wine

1½ teaspoons salt

Several sprigs of fresh thyme

½ cup Niçoise or Gaeta olives

In a large skillet, heat 2 tablespoons oil over medium high heat. Brown the meat in batches, adding 1 more tablespoon oil to brown the last batch of meat. Transfer it to a 9-quart dutch oven.

In the same skillet, sauté the onions over medium heat for 3 minutes, shaking the pan occasionally.

Add the onions, the uncooked mushrooms, and the garlic cloves to the meat. Stir in the tomato sauce and wine; sprinkle with salt and add the thyme.

Cover and braise over low heat for 3 hours, stirring occasionally. The braising juices should barely quiver during the cooking and to keep the meat moist, no steam should escape. If it does, lower the heat.

Scatter the olives and cook for another 15 minutes.

Boeuf en casserole des mariniers du Rhône

Beef Shanks Braised in Onions from the Bargemen of the Rhone

MY FATHER WAS a bargeman until he met my mother, when he gave it up. His son from a first marriage continued the family tradition of barging. I spent many happy days on my brother's barge, plying the northern canals of France. Many years later when I saw this dish in a local restaurant near Nyons, I had to try it.

It's a very simple dish, without broth, wine, or water; but it needs a pot with a tight-fitting lid. If you don't own such a pot, buy an inexpensive black cast-iron dutch oven with a glass lid at the hardware store.

The meat cooks very, very slowly in the liquid exuded by the onions. The humidity that gathers on the underside of the lid of the pot will fall back into the pan to make more pan juices.

With this dish, I serve Sautéed Young Turnips (page 234) and steamed potatoes.

SERVES 4 TO 6

1 teaspoon olive oil

4 slices of beef shank, 1½ inches thick, bone in and fat trimmed (about 4 pounds)

2 pounds onions, sliced

2½ teaspoons salt

Freshly ground black pepper

3 sprigs of fresh thyme

5 sprigs of parsley

4 anchovy fillets in oil, patted dry

4 large garlic cloves

Preheat the oven to 300 degrees.

Oil the bottom of a dutch oven large enough to comfortably fit the meat in 1 layer. Put half the onion slices on the bottom of the pan and sprinkle with 1 teaspoon salt. Nestle the meat on top. Sprinkle with ½ teaspoon salt and freshly ground pepper, add the fresh thyme, and cover with the remaining onion slices; sprinkle with the remaining salt. Cover tightly.

Braise for 3 hours in the oven.

In the bowl of a food processor, process the parsley, anchovies, and garlic until smooth. Set aside.

Transfer the meat and onions to a serving bowl; degrease the pan juices and pour over the meat. Serve with the parsley-anchovy mixture on the side (substitute horseradish if you don't like anchovies).

Raviolis niçoises

Ravioli from Nice

IN NICE, WHERE French ravioli originate, the stuffing consists of meat leftovers from a beef stew, spinach, lamb brains, and cheese. I have omitted the brains.

I have friends who make beef stew only to make these ravioli. It's a lot of work for 1 person, which is why I invite friends over who like to cook, to help out.

Ravioli freeze well, so make a large batch for several dinners. If I don't have enough cooking juices left from a stew, I substitute 1-Hour Rich Broth (page 12).

MAKES ABOUT 5½ DOZEN 2½-INCH RAVIOLI

2 pounds young spinach leaves

1½ tablespoons olive oil

2 tablespoons sour cream

½ teaspoon salt

Pinch of nutmeg

3 cups minced cooked meat (from beef stews, pages 152, 154, or 158)

1 egg yolk

8 tablespoons grated Parmesan cheese or more

1 pound Fresh Egg Pasta (page 31)

2 cups leftover beef stew pan juices or more

or 2 cups 1-Hour Rich Broth or more (page 12)

Wash the spinach, discarding the large stems, but do not spin dry.

Over low heat cook the spinach in a large pan, covered, until wilted, about 5 minutes. Drain and refresh the spinach under cold running water. Squeeze it to eliminate as much moisture as possible.

Puree the spinach in a food processor; you should have a little more than 1 cup.

In a nonstick skillet, heat the oil over medium heat. Add the spinach and sour cream; sprinkle with ½ teaspoon salt and a pinch of nutmeg. Cook for 3 minutes, stirring occasionally, until the liquid is evaporated.

In the food processor, process the meat, spinach, egg yolk, and ⅓ cup grated Parmesan cheese for 30 seconds. Mix in more Parmesan if the stuffing is too loose.

Roll out the pasta dough according to the instructions on page 33.

Stamp out 2½-inch circles from the pasta sheets. Cover them with a damp towel to keep the dough from drying out.

Mound a little less than 1 tablespoon meat stuffing on half the circles and cover them with the remaining halves. Tightly seal the edges, pushing down with the back of the tines of a fork.

Transfer them to a towel sprinkled with cornmeal. (The ravioli can be frozen at this point. Freeze on a cookie sheet. When frozen, place the ravioli in a freezer bag.)

In a large saucepan, boil 2 quarts salted water. Add the ravioli (fresh or frozen) and bring back to a light boil. Boil for 10 minutes. Test for doneness by tasting one.

Preheat the oven to 350 degrees.

Drain the ravioli in a fine-meshed strainer and transfer them to a greased 3-quart baking dish.

Pour 2 cups or more of leftover beef stew juices or rich broth over the ravioli and sprinkle 2 tablespoons grated Parmesan on top.

Bake in the middle shelf of the oven for 10 minutes.

Set the broiler on high and gratiné the top for a minute.

Pot au feu du Midi

Boiled Dinner from the South

I INVITE GOOD friends for this simple feast. In the Midi, lamb is one of the *pot au feu* meats. I also make it with shanks of beef and veal. At serving time, I mound the shanks, their large marrow bones, and vegetables on a wooden platter surrounded by small bowls of Provençal condiments (these prepared ahead of time): aioli, spicy tomato sauce, grated carrot salad, mustard, and capers.

It's such a simple dish that I never make it ahead of time (it tastes better freshly made), and I bake baguettes to serve hot from the oven along with the *pot au feu*.

SERVES 6 TO 8

½ beef shank (4 pounds with bone in)

1 whole veal shank (2½ to 3 pounds)

2 lamb shanks (3 pounds)

A bouquet garni (bouquet of parsley tied with 1 young tender branch of celery with leaves and several sprigs of fresh thyme or 1 teaspoon dry thyme wrapped in cheesecloth)

2 tablespoons salt

6 large carrots, peeled

6 medium leeks, greens discarded, washed and tied together

1 large onion

One 28-ounce can plum tomatoes, juice strained (and reserved for a soup)

2 pounds Yukon Gold or any all-purpose potatoes, peeled and cut into 2-inch cubes (6 cups)

Aioli (page 104)

Spicy Tomato Sauce (page 10)

A small bowl of Niçoise or Gaeta olives

A small bowl of capers

A small bowl of sea salt

A small bowl of hot mustard and/or a small bowl of grated horseradish

Grated Carrot Salad (page 52)

In a 10-quart stockpot, cover the meats with 15 cups water. Bring the water to a light boil over medium heat; it should take about 25 minutes, and skim off the scum that rises.

When the froth on top of the boiling water is clear, add 1 more cup of water, bouquet garni, and salt.

Partially cover and simmer, keeping the broth at a light boil for 1 hour.

Add the carrots, leeks, onion, and tomatoes. If the vegetables are not totally covered with broth, don't worry, just submerge them as best as you can. Partially cover and simmer, keeping the broth at a light boil for 1½ hours.

A half hour before serving, cover the potatoes with salted cold water. Bring to a boil, partially cover, and cook for 20 minutes or until tender.

Transfer the meat, bones, and vegetables to a platter with the potatoes. Discard the bouquet garni.

Bring the broth back to a boil and discard the fat, skimming with a ladle to remove it.

Serve a large bowl of broth and bowls of aioli, spicy tomato sauce, olives, capers, sea salt, hot mustard, and grated carrots with the meats and vegetables.

On Veal Breast

IN FRANCE, THE *tendrons* are the last ribs of the rib cage (veal breast) of a calf, just before the real veal chops; they are also called the poor man's chops. In the States, I ask that the center cut of the veal breast be cut into "spareribs"; you can substitute veal chops or osso bucco. In winter, I cook the veal with homemade tomato sauce, and in summer with fresh tomatoes; the dishes are made in advance and reheated before serving.

Tendrons de veau poêle à la dioise

Veal Breast Spareribs with Fresh Tomatoes

LUCIENNE GONNET, my butcher's wife in Luc-en-Diois, cooks this dish during the summer at the peak of tomato season. Out of season, she substitutes 3 cups of tomato sauce (page 8 or page 10) and 1 teaspoon dried thyme if fresh basil is unavailable.

Ask the butcher to cut the breast meat parallel to the bones into strips just like veal spareribs, and each sparerib into 3 pieces crosswise. Trim as much fat as possible without breaking up the pieces.

In summer, I serve Pan-Fried Eggplants and Peppers with Garlic (page 205) and off season I serve Fresh Egg Pasta (page 31).

SERVES 6

4 pounds veal breast, cut into 4-inch-long and 2-inch-wide spareribs, fat trimmed

Flour for dredging

3 tablespoons olive oil

1 teaspoon salt

Freshly ground black pepper

2 medium onions, sliced (2 cups)

3 large garlic cloves, coarsely chopped

½ cup basil leaves

2 pounds fresh tomatoes, peeled, seeded, and cut into cubes (4 cups) (see Note, page 9)

Dredge several "spareribs" in flour, shaking off the excess.

In a large nonstick skillet, heat the oil over medium high heat. Brown the meat in batches, turning it over to brown evenly.

Transfer the meat to a 9-quart dutch oven. Sprinkle with ½ teaspoon salt and freshly ground pepper.

In the same skillet, cook the onions over low to medium heat for 5 minutes, stirring occasionally. Transfer to the dutch oven.

In a food processor, process the garlic cloves, remaining salt, and basil for a minute.

Scatter the tomatoes and the garlic and basil mixture over the meat and onions. Cover tightly and cook for 2 hours over medium heat, stirring the meat and vegetables occasionally.

Set aside to cool. Discard the fat before reheating

Tendrons de veau grillés

Grilled Veal Spareribs with Lemon and Fresh Mint

ASK THE BUTCHER to bone the veal breast and to slice it into boneless spareribs. With the grilled veal, I like to serve ratatouille (pages 229, 236, or 238).

SERVES 6

Six 2-inch-wide and 10-inch-long boned veal spareribs, fat trimmed

¼ cup olive oil

½ cup freshly squeezed lemon juice

5 large garlic cloves, minced

½ teaspoon salt

Freshly ground black pepper

1 teaspoon minced mint

Coil the veal and secure the coils crosswise with a skewer. Place them side by side in a shallow pan.

In a small bowl, combine the oil, lemon juice, and garlic and sprinkle with ½ teaspoon salt and freshly ground pepper.

Pour 1 tablespoon of the sauce over each coil of meat and set aside for 1 hour.

Heat a bed of coals to medium hot in the barbecue. Grill the meat about 15 minutes, turning it once. Occasionally, baste with the lemon sauce. Make a small incision in the meat to test for doneness.

Scatter the minced mint over the meat and serve.

Blanquette de veau du Midi

Veal Stew from the South

Blanquette de veau, a favorite stew among the French, is often served with steamed potatoes or Fresh Egg Pasta (page 31).

SERVES 6

4 pounds veal breast, cut into 4-inch-long and 2-inch-wide spareribs, fat trimmed

1 cup dry white wine

1 large onion, quartered

4 cloves

A bouquet garni (bouquet of parsley tied with 1 tender celery branch with leaves and 2 sprigs of fresh thyme or 1 teaspoon dry thyme wrapped in cheesecloth and 1 bay leaf)

2 garlic cloves

1 teaspoon whole black peppercorns

2 teaspoons salt

3 tablespoons olive oil

3 tablespoons flour

FOR THE PERSILLADE

2 tablespoons minced parsley

1 teaspoon minced garlic

Place the veal, 5 cups water, and the wine in a 6-quart dutch oven. Bring it slowly to a boil. Skim and discard the scum as it rises to the surface. Add the onion stuck with cloves, bouquet garni, garlic, peppercorns, and salt.

Simmer over medium heat, uncovered, for 45 minutes. Drain the meat, reserving the broth (yields about 3 cups of broth). Discard the bouquet garni. Pat the meat dry with paper towels.

Degrease the broth if necessary and boil it down gently while you brown the meat.

In a large nonstick skillet, heat the oil over medium high heat. Brown the meat, turning it to brown evenly. Sprinkle with the flour and sauté the meat until the flour turns light brown, about 15 minutes.

Add 2 cups of broth. Cover and simmer for 1 hour, basting once in a while and adding more broth when the sauce becomes too thick. (Can be done ahead of time.)

Reheat the meat, sprinkle with garlic and parsley, and serve.

Jarrets de veau en cocotte aux petits oignons

Veal Shanks Braised with Pearl Onions and Tarragon

ORDER THE SHANKS ahead of time, otherwise butchers display them already cut for osso bucco. The shanks are roasted whole.

Serve with Potato Puffs (page 218).

SERVES 6

1½ cups pearl onions

1 tablespoon olive oil

Two 2½-pound veal shanks
(each shank weighs 2½
pounds)

2 sprigs of fresh tarragon

1 teaspoon salt

Freshly ground black pepper

Spinach Garnish (see below)

Plunge the onions in 2 quarts boiling water for 1 minute. Drain and rinse under cold water. Peel.

In a large nonstick skillet, heat the oil over medium high heat. Brown the veal shanks, turning them on all sides, about 15 minutes. Transfer them to a 6-quart dutch oven.

Scatter the onions around the shanks, add the sprigs of tarragon, and sprinkle with salt and freshly ground pepper. Pour ½ cup water into the pan, cover tightly, and cook over low heat on top of the stove (the pan juices should barely quiver) for 45 minutes, turning the shanks occasionally.

Turn off the heat and set aside for 15 minutes.

Transfer the meat to a wooden cutting board with a groove to catch the juices. Holding the shank bone straight up, cut thin slices of meat parallel to the bone.

Reheat the pan juices and onions with the juices from the cutting board. Boil the juices for 2 minutes. Taste and correct seasoning.

Serve the veal on a bed of spinach, and ladle the sauce on top. Serve immediately.

Garniture d'épinards

SPINACH GARNISH

MAKES 1½ CUPS

2 pounds young spinach leaves

1 teaspoon salt

½ cup milk or more

⅛ teaspoon grated nutmeg

Freshly ground black pepper

Wash the spinach under running cold water, discarding the stems. Turn into a large saucepan, cover, and cook over medium heat for 10 minutes. Sprinkle with salt after 5 minutes.

Drain the spinach and refresh under the tap. Squeeze out the liquid.

In the food processor, puree the spinach, pouring the milk through the chute (add more milk if the puree is too dry).

In a medium saucepan, reheat the spinach. Sprinkle with the nutmeg and freshly ground pepper. Taste and correct seasoning.

Jarrets de veau au fenouil

Osso Bucco with Fennel, Capers, and Lime

THIS IS MY students' favorite dish. In class, we serve Old-Fashioned Mashed Potatoes (page 222) or White Bean Puree (page 243) with the osso bucco.

SERVES 6

¼ cup olive oil

4 pounds veal shanks, cut into 1½-inch-thick slices

Flour for dredging

2 onions, chopped coarsely (2 cups)

1½ cups coarsely chopped fennel bulb

1 teaspoon salt

Freshly ground black pepper

1½ cups Chardonnay

½ cup Niçoise or Gaeta olives

1 tablespoon drained capers

1 small lime, thinly sliced

In a large nonstick skillet, heat 2 tablespoons oil over medium high heat. Dredge the slices of osso bucco in flour, shaking off the excess, and quickly brown them evenly on all sides, including bottom and top. Set aside.

In the same skillet, cook the onions over low heat for 5 minutes, occasionally stirring. Remove the onions to a plate.

Add the remaining oil to the skillet and cook the fennel for 5 minutes.

Scatter half the onions and fennel at the bottom of a 9-quart dutch oven, add the osso bucco, sprinkle with salt and pepper, and scatter the remaining onions and fennel on top of the meat.

Pour the wine over the meat. Cover and simmer over low heat for 1½ hours, checking once in a while to make sure the pan juices do not evaporate too fast.

For the last 15 minutes of cooking, scatter the olives, capers, and lime on top of the osso bucco.

Ris de veau au romarin et aux citrons confits

Sweetbreads with Rosemary and Preserved Lemons

THE DISH CAN be prepared on the afternoon of the dinner party.

If you don't have time to preserve lemons, you can buy them in specialty stores or eliminate them from the recipe but do not substitute fresh lemons, which would be too acidic. I like to serve Braised Carrots with Fresh Herbs (page 199) or Mashed Potatoes with Goat Cheese (page 221).

SERVES 6

2 pounds veal sweetbreads

6 small sprigs of rosemary

1 teaspoon lemon juice

2 tablespoons butter

Freshly ground black pepper

12 wedges Preserved Lemons (page 14)

2 cups 1-Hour Rich Broth (page 12) (optional)

Cover the sweetbreads with cold water. Slowly bring the water to a boil. Boil for 1 minute. Drain. Rinse under cold running water. Set aside to cool.

Remove only the most visible membranes and tough cartilage; do not remove any fine membrane or the sweetbreads will fall apart.

Cut the sweetbreads into 6 equal portions. With the point of a knife, make 1 incision in each sweetbread and stick in a small cluster of rosemary. Sprinkle with lemon juice and cover for 1 hour.

In a 6-quart dutch oven, melt butter over medium heat. Sauté the sweetbreads until golden brown, about 5 minutes, turning gently. Season with freshly ground pepper.

Discard the pulp of the preserved lemons and scatter the rinds on top of the sweetbreads. Cover and braise for 30 minutes.

Transfer the sweetbreads and the lemon rinds to a preheated platter. The sweetbreads can be served as is without a sauce.

Or pour the rich broth in the pan and boil down to 1 cup, skimming the surface fat.

L AMB

LAMB IS THE most popular meat in the Midi. Jean Giono, the writer and poet of northern Provence, immortalized the transhumance, the seasonal migration of herds of sheep, shepherds, and sheep dogs to their summer homes, high on top of the Alps of Provence. It's a sight to behold the masses of sheep parading through towns and villages, cheered on by the villagers, who drink to the health of the shepherds!

French lamb are slaughtered very young. A leg weighs about 4 pounds; an American leg of lamb weighs 7 to 8 pounds. To make cooking easier I ask my New York butcher to separate the leg into 2 parts: the pelvic and the shank, each weighing about 3½ pounds. With the leftovers, make Tomatoes Stuffed with Lamb (page 172) and freeze the bones and the meat still on them for a broth (page 12).

Gigot d'agneau rôti

Roast Leg of Lamb

THIS SAVORY LEG of lamb is as good as a plain roast, but close to perfect when paired with the White Bean Stew.

SERVES 8

7 to 8 pounds leg of lamb, cut into the shank and the pelvic portions, fat trimmed

2 teaspoons olive oil

1 teaspoon salt

Freshly ground pepper

White Bean Stew (page 244) (optional)

Preheat the oven to 450 degrees.

Brush the meat with olive oil. Place it on a rack and put the rack on top of a 3-quart roasting pan or baking dish.

Roast for 20 minutes. Lower the heat to 400 degrees. Sprinkle with salt and freshly ground pepper.

If you are making the bean stew, pour the beans and liquid into the roasting pan, add 1 cup water, and stir. Place the rack with the lamb on top of the pan.

With or without the beans, roast in the middle of the oven for 45 minutes.

Set aside the leg of lamb for 15 minutes before carving.

With beans, continue cooking them while the roast is resting.

Serve slices of lamb on top of the beans or without the beans. I serve the roast of lamb with Tomatoes à la Provençale (page 232).

Tomates farcies à l'agneau

Tomatoes Stuffed with Lamb

JULIETTE RASCLARD, who is one of my best sources for real country cooking, makes superb stuffed tomatoes with leftover lamb and cheese. The tomatoes and basil come from her garden, she makes her own goat cheese, and the lamb is supplied by her brother-in-law, who slaughters lamb in the Hautes-Alpes; no wonder her stuffed tomatoes are fabulous.

Summer is the best time to make this dish because tomatoes are at their peak; in the States, I substitute feta cheese for the goat cheese.

The stuffed tomatoes are always better made a day in advance.

SERVES 4

Eight 5-ounce fresh tomatoes

$1^1/2$ teaspoons salt

$^1/2$ cup shredded fresh basil

12 ounces leftover lamb, coarsely chopped (2 cups)

1 medium onion, coarsely chopped

4 large garlic cloves, coarsely chopped

3 tablespoons olive oil

$^1/2$ cup grated goat cheese or feta

Freshly ground black pepper

Preheat the oven to 350 degrees.

Slice 1 inch off the end of the tomatoes opposite the stem side and reserve.

Scoop out the tomato pulp and reserve (yields about $1^1/4$ cups). Sprinkle the inside of the tomatoes with $^1/2$ teaspoon salt, turn them over, and place them on a rack.

Process the pulp with the basil in a food processor. Set aside.

In a large bowl, mix the meat, onion, and garlic; make 2 piles. Pulse each pile about a dozen times in a food processor (yields approximatively 3 cups in all).

In a large nonstick skillet, heat 2 tablespoons oil over medium high heat. Brown the meat mixture for 5 minutes, stirring occasionally.

Add the tomato pulp, cheese, 1 teaspoon salt, and freshly ground pepper. Cook for 10 minutes or until the liquid evaporates.

Place the tomatoes in an oiled 9½-inch-square baking dish; overfill each tomato with the meat and tomato mixture and cover with the reserved tomato tops.

Gently prick the body of the tomatoes with the point of a knife. Dribble 1 tablespoon olive oil over the tomatoes.

Bake for 1 hour, basting occasionally. Serve hot.

If made in advance, reheat just before serving in a 300-degree preheated oven for 15 minutes.

Carré d'agneau du Tricastin

Rack of Lamb with Potatoes and Rosemary

THE TRICASTIN, a region north of Orange in the valley east of the Rhone, is famous for its lamb and its vineyards.

For this recipe, the rack should be frenched, which means trimming the fat and removing a second thin layer of meat on top of the eye of the rack and scraping the bones of the chops clean of fat and bits of meat.

Before trimming, a rack weighs 2 to 3 pounds, and after frenching, it weighs around 1 pound. Ask for the trimmings, discard the fat from them, and reserve for a rich broth (page 12).

There's not much meat on a rack of lamb, so when I serve one for a dinner party, I make sure to have a first course like Country Onion Tart (page 89) and a gutsy vegetable course such as Ratatouille Terrine (page 225).

There are about 8 chops; I serve 2 per person.

SERVES 4

2 pounds all-purpose potatoes
(Yukon Gold, Long White) cut
into 1/2-inch cubes
(5 to 6 cups)

1 pound frenched rack of lamb

1 sprig of rosemary

1/3 cup olive oil

1/3 cup minced fresh parsley

3 large garlic cloves, minced

1 teaspoon salt

Freshly ground black pepper

Bring a large amount of salted water to a boil. Add the potatoes and boil until tender, about 6 to 10 minutes after the water reboils. Drain and rinse under cold water and set aside.

Preheat the oven to 500 degrees or prepare hot coals in a barbecue (see opposite).

Oil the bottom of a 9-inch black iron skillet and add the rack, placing a sprig of rosemary on top.

Roast on the top rack of the oven for 15 minutes.

Transfer the meat to a cutting board. Set aside for 15 minutes.

In a large nonstick skillet heat the oil and sauté the potatoes, stirring, in 2 batches until lightly browned.

Mix the parsley and garlic. Sprinkle it over the potatoes and sauté 1 more minute. Sprinkle with salt and freshly ground pepper.

Carve the rack into individual chops. Serve immediately with the potatoes.

On Barbecuing

I USE AN American-made barbecue with a cover and small adjustable air-intake holes for barbecuing; these two features permit close control of the timing and the degree of char.

Use plenty of real wood charcoal, for best flavor and uniform heat.

Start the fire 20 to 30 minutes before cooking.

Have the meat at room temperature.

Once the coals are uniformly glowing (shift them with tongs if need be), put the meat on, over the red coals, and sear the outside without burning it.

Remove the meat from the grill.

Cover the barbecue, reduce the draft, and allow the coals to whiten with ash, about 4 to 5 minutes.

Add 3 to 4 large sprigs of fresh rosemary or sage to the coals and transfer the meat back to the grill. Cover immediately so the herb sprigs don't catch fire.

Grill the meat about 7 minutes and turn it over for 4 to 5 minutes. You must peek at it every now and again to make sure it's not burning. Squirt on a little water if flames start to lick the meat.

Set the meat aside for 10 minutes before slicing.

Rôti de selle d'agneau désossée

Boned Roast Saddle of Lamb

ASK THE BUTCHER to bone, trim the fat, and tie a saddle of lamb. Reserve the bones to make 1-Hour Rich Broth. To vary, I stuff the lamb with spinach and cheese (see Variation). Simply roasted, I serve the saddle with Gratin of Eggplants with Red Pepper and Feta cheese (page 201); with the stuffed saddle I serve Onion and Morel Gratin (page 213).

SERVES 8

1 tablespoon olive oil

3½ pounds boned and tied saddle
    of lamb, fat trimmed

Salt

Freshly ground black pepper

1 cup 1-Hour Rich Broth (page 12)

2 tablespoons butter

Preheat the oven to 425 degrees.

Heat a large black iron skillet and coat with olive oil.

Over very high heat, sear the roast on all sides until it is golden brown, about 7 minutes. Season with salt and freshly ground black pepper.

Discard the fat in the skillet.

Roast the lamb in the middle of the oven for 30 minutes for medium-rare lamb, turning the roast after 15 minutes and discarding fat.

Set aside for 15 minutes. Transfer the roast to a grooved cutting board and carve into ½-inch slices.

In a large skillet, heat the rich broth with the juice that dribbles out of the roast.

Whisk in butter and boil for 1 more minute. Serve the sauce in a warmed sauceboat to accompany the lamb.

Rôti de selle d'agneau farcie

ROASTED STUFFED SADDLE OF LAMB

I MAKE THIS spinach stuffing for omelets, crepes, and mushroom caps as well as for stuffing a roast. I always make more than I need so I have leftovers, which I freeze. If you want to make just enough for this saddle of lamb, make half the recipe.

SERVES 8

1 tablespoon olive oil

1 medium onion, sliced

1 large garlic clove, sliced

1 pound fresh young spinach

1 teaspoon salt

1 egg

$^1\!/_4$ cup fresh ricotta cheese

$^1\!/_3$ cup grated Parmesan cheese

$^1\!/_3$ cup coarse fresh bread crumbs

1 teaspoon fresh thyme leaves

$3^1\!/_2$ pounds boned and tied saddle of lamb, fat trimmed

In a nonstick skillet, heat the oil over medium high heat. Cook the onion and garlic for 5 minutes, stirring occasionally. Set aside.

Discard the spinach stems and wash the leaves thoroughly but do not spin dry. Add to a 3-quart saucepan and cover. Cook over medium heat for 5 minutes until wilted. Uncover, raise the heat to high, and stir constantly until the liquid has evaporated. Set aside to cool in a colander, then squeeze the spinach to remove remaining liquid.

In the bowl of a food processor, process the onion and garlic, spinach, salt, egg, ricotta, Parmesan, bread crumbs, and thyme. Taste and correct seasoning.

Refrigerate until cold, about 1 hour.

Untie the saddle. Spread the stuffing on the underside of the saddle and roll it back to its original shape. Tie with string every $^1\!/_2$ inch.

Proceed as for Boned Roast Saddle of Lamb, opposite.

Rouelles d'agneau à l'arlésienne

Osso Bucco of Lamb Shanks with Tomatoes and Garlic from Arles

I MAKE THIS dish only when tomatoes are in season; I also make it in advance because the meat becomes more flavorful as it sits. I serve Fava Bean Puree (page 206), White Bean Puree (page 243), or Onion and Morel Gratin (page 213) with the osso bucco.

SERVES 6

2 tablespoons olive oil

4 lamb shanks, cut crosswise into
    1½-inch-thick slices

10 large garlic cloves, peeled and
    crushed

1½ pounds fresh tomatoes, peeled,
    seeded, and chopped (3 cups)
    (see Note, page 9)

½ cup shredded basil leaves

1 teaspoon salt

Freshly ground black pepper

In a 6-quart dutch oven, heat the oil over medium high heat. Brown the lamb osso bucco, turning it occasionally, about 10 to 15 minutes.

Scatter the garlic, the tomatoes, and basil around the lamb. Sprinkle with salt and freshly ground pepper; add ¼ cup water.

Cover and braise 1½ hours over medium heat on top of the stove.

Discard the surface fat and reheat the shanks before serving.

Tian d'agneau aux aubergines

Provençal Moussaka

IF THERE ARE meat leftovers in Provençal kitchens, chances are it will be lamb. Moussaka is the answer to these leftovers. Though it takes time to prepare, its flavor develops well if it's cooked a day or two ahead of serving.

It is important for the success of the dish that you buy long, slim eggplants.

SERVES 8

5 eggplants (4 pounds), each 10 inches long

6 tablespoons olive oil

1 pound leftover lamb, coarsely chopped (2½ cups)

2 tablespoons minced garlic

1½ teaspoons salt

Freshly ground black pepper

3 pounds fresh tomatoes, peeled and cut into ¼-inch-thick slices (6 cups)

1 tablespoon fresh thyme leaves

2 cups Spicy Tomato Sauce (page 10)

Sprigs of fresh thyme (optional)

¼ cup Niçoise or Gaeta olives

Oil a high layer cake pan, 10 inches wide and 2 inches deep.

Preheat the broiler to high for 10 minutes and place the oven rack 5 inches from the heating element.

Slice 4 eggplants lengthwise into ¼-inch slices. Brush 2 tablespoons olive oil over both sides and broil lightly, turning the eggplant slices once; it takes about 6 to 7 minutes in all.

Bring 3 quarts of water to a boil in a 5-quart pot.

Cut the remaining eggplant into ¼-inch slices crosswise. Boil them for 5 minutes or until soft. Drain and set aside.

In a large nonstick skillet, heat 2 tablespoons oil over medium high heat. Brown the lamb with the garlic for 3 to 4 minutes. Sprinkle with ½ teaspoon salt and freshly ground pepper. Transfer to a bowl.

continued

In the same skillet, heat 2 more tablespoons oil over high heat. Sauté the tomato slices in 2 batches for 2 minutes each, stirring. Set aside.

Preheat the oven to 400 degrees.

Line the bottom and sides of the prepared cake pan with the broiled eggplant slices, making a cartwheel design, hanging 1 end of the slices over the side of the pan.

Layer the tomatoes on top of the eggplant slices, sprinkle with $^1/_2$ teaspoon salt, freshly ground pepper, and 1 teaspoon thyme leaves.

Spread the chopped meat on the tomatoes. Sprinkle with 1 teaspoon thyme leaves and cover with $^1/_2$ cup tomato sauce.

Layer the boiled eggplant slices, saving a few slices to cover the top of the mold; sprinkle with $^1/_2$ teaspoon salt, freshly ground pepper, and the remaining thyme leaves. Cover with $^1/_2$ cup tomato sauce.

Fold the overhanging eggplant slices over the tomato sauce and cover with the remaining slices of eggplant if necessary to cover any gaps.

Cover the pan with foil. Fit the pan in a large skillet. Pour enough water into the skillet to come halfway up the sides of the mold.

Bake 30 minutes.

Set aside for 5 minutes to cool, pushing down on the cake. Serve as is in the mold or unmold on a cake platter and decorate with fresh thyme sprigs.

Serve with the reserved tomato sauce heated with black olives.

The tian can be reheated in a water bath (a skillet is fine) at 400 degrees for 15 minutes.

Pork

Joel Aubert, my grandfather, was too poor to raise a pig. His chicken, his sheep, and Bijoune, the mule, were easy to feed but a pig was another matter. He did not have enough table scraps even to make a soup for the pig. For years in the back hills of the Drôme, owning a pig was a sign of wealth. In early winter, when they butchered their pigs, the Oddons and Ponsons, his neighbors, always gave my grandfather a Christmas gift of pâtés, sausages, and *petit salé* (unsmoked bacon in preserved salt).

Today, we can easily go to a butcher and buy fresh pork, but the tradition remains in the Drôme to cook with preserved pork.

When the hunting season starts, every hunter is ready to hunt for wild boars; the hills of the south Drôme are a natural habitat. The hunters' wives then prepare delicious wild boar stews (see page 143) served with polenta.

Saucisses et haricots blancs à la villageoise

Country Village Sausage and Beans

WHEN I COOK this dish in New York, I buy kielbasas and fresh bacon with the rind. In Nyons, I buy *petit salé*, lightly salted unsmoked bacon, and *saucisses à l'ail*, fresh garlic sausage.

SERVES 6 TO 8

1½ pounds dry white beans, cannelini, Great Northern, or navy

1 pound kielbasa, cut up in 6 pieces

2 tablespoons olive oil

2 onions, minced (2 cups)

4 garlic cloves

One 14-ounce can Italian plum tomatoes (juice saved for a soup)

1 pound fresh bacon with rind, cut in 6 pieces

5 teaspoons salt

Freshly ground black pepper

Pinch of nutmeg

3 sprigs of thyme

1 bay leaf

Soak the beans overnight in a large amount of water.

Drain the beans. In a 9-quart dutch oven, cover the beans with water and bring to a boil. Drain.

In a medium pan, cover the kielbasa pieces with cold water. Bring to a boil and boil 5 minutes to reduce the smoky flavor of the kielbasa. Drain and refresh under running cold water. Set aside.

In the dutch oven, heat the olive oil over medium heat. Add the onions and garlic. Cover and braise for 5 minutes.

Uncover, add the tomatoes, and cook for 5 minutes over medium high heat, stirring occasionally.

continued

Add the beans and stir. Bury the sausage and fresh bacon in the beans. Pour in 4 cups water.

Braise over low heat for 2 hours. After 30 minutes, stir in the salt, pepper, and nutmeg. Add the thyme and bay leaf. Check occasionally to make sure some liquid remains in the pot; the beans should be moist.

Serve directly from the dutch oven with a crusty bread and lots of Côtes du Rhône.

Épaule de porc braisée au romarin et à l'ail

Braised Pork Shoulder with Rosemary and Garlic

GEORGETTE ODDON, my friend and neighbor in Brézès, near Valdrôme, keeps her wood stove going for cooking even in the summer. First she browns meat or fowl, then she covers it, and leaves it all morning on top of the stove, closing the damper of the stove so the food will not burn; it also permits the meat to slowly braise. It's as simple as that.

Serve with Old-Fashioned Mashed Potatoes (page 222) or Pumpkin Gratin (page 223).

SERVES 8

2 tablespoons Dijon mustard

6 pounds pork shoulder, fat and rind removed

2 tablespoons olive oil

8 garlic cloves, peeled

1 teaspoon salt

Freshly ground black pepper

2 sprigs of rosemary

Smear the mustard on the pork.

In a 6-quart dutch oven, heat the oil over medium high heat. Brown the pork on all sides, being careful not to burn the mustard; this takes about 30 minutes. Add the garlic cloves for the last 5 minutes of browning.

Sprinkle salt and freshly ground pepper over the meat. Add sprigs of rosemary. Cover tightly and simmer for $2^{1}/_{2}$ hours. Peek inside the pan occasionally, letting the condensation gathered on the underside of the lid drip back into the pan.

Transfer the meat to a carving board. Boil down the braising juices to about 1 cup, if necessary, and serve the braising juices in a sauceboat.

Grillade d'échine de porc à la sauge

Barbecued Pork Shoulder Steaks

IN THE EARLY 1970s, I shopped in Die (pronounced "Dee," not "Dye"), the home of Clairette de Die, a crisp and refreshing sparkling wine. (A wine merchant tried to sell it in New York without any success because of its name.) I bought *échine de porc*, pork shoulder roast, for barbecuing from Kiki, a butcher in Die who I thought was the best. One day, I asked Kiki to cut the roast into 1/2-inch-thick slices.

"What on earth for?" he asked.

I told him we grilled the meat on a barbecue. "Impossible," said Kiki. "Why don't you try it?" I challenged. Next week, a sign in Kiki's window announced GRILLADE DE PORC—with a price increase. *Grillade de porc* is everywhere in the Drôme and Vaucluse regions and I'm happy to take credit for it!

Pork shoulder has lots of fat and bone to give it flavor and keep it moist and juicy in cooking.

Serve the meat with 15-Minute Ratatouille (page 229) or Spinach in a Béchamel with Hard-Boiled Eggs and Croutons (page 230).

SERVES 4

Four 1/2-inch slices of pork   2 to 3 sprigs of sage
   shoulder chops, fat trimmed

Prepare a fire in the barbecue according to the instructions on page 179. The meat cooks quickly, so you don't need a long-burning fire.

When the coals are red hot, sear the meat on both sides. This will create lots of smoke but don't worry. Remove the meat.

Reduce the draft, add the sage sprigs to the coals, let the coals whiten, and put the meat back on the rack.

Keep an eye on the meat: when pale red juices start to form on the top of the slices, turn them, about 3 to 4 minutes, depending on the coals. Keep a squirt gun handy to put out flare-ups.

Grill the other side (4 minutes). Remove the pieces of meat one by one, as they get done; the meat is uneven so the slices cook at different rates.

Test with a sharp-pointed knife for doneness. I prefer this pork a little pink, but most people are scared of trichinosis and like it cooked to whiteness clear through.

Vegetables, Beans, and Grains

Artichokes

Artichauts en ragoût • 195
(Stew of Baby Artichokes with White Onions and Garlic)

Jerusalem Artichokes (Sun Chokes)

Topinambours à la provençale • 196
(Ragout of Jerusalem Artichokes à la Provençale)

Cabbage

Chartreuse de chou • 197
(Cabbage Chartreuse)

Carrots

Carottes braisées aux herbes • 199
(Braised Carrots with Fresh Herbs)

Eggplants

Tian d'aubergines du Comtat Venaissin • 200
(Eggplant Gratin from the Vaucluse)

Tian d'aubergines et de poivrons rouges au fromage • 201
(Gratin of Eggplants with Red Peppers and Feta Cheese)

Gratin d'aubergines Uzès • 203
(Eggplant Gratin Uzès)

Sauté d'aubergines et de poivrons à l'ail • 205
(Pan-Fried Eggplants and Peppers with Garlic)

Fava Beans

Purée de fèves • 206
   (Fava Bean Puree)

Fennel

Fenouil rôti • 207
   (Roasted Fennel)

Fondue de fenouil • 208
   (Fondue of Fennel)

Green Peas

Petits pois à la française • 209
   (Peas Braised with Salad Greens)

Purée de petits pois à l'ail • 210
   (Green Pea Puree with Garlic)

Mushrooms

Confit de pommes de terre et barigoules • 211
   (Confit of Potatoes with Wild Mushrooms)

Gratin d'oignons et morilles • 213
   (Onion and Morel Gratin)

Girolles braisées à l'ail et aux échalotes • 215
   (Braised Chanterelles with Garlic and Shallots)

Les Cèpes farcies • 216
   (Stuffed Porcini Caps)

Potatoes, Onions, and Endives

Croquettes de pommes de terre • 218
   (Potato Puffs)

Gratin de pommes de terre au fromage • 220
   (Scalloped Potatoes with Cheese)

Zucchini

Courgettes poêlées, à l'ail et au gruyère • 235
    (Pan-Fried Zucchini with Garlic and Gruyère)

Gratin de courgettes épicées • 236
    (Spicy Zucchini Gratin)

Gratin de courgettes aux oignons • 237
    (Squash and Onion Gratin)

Cornmeal and Semolina

Soufflé de polenta • 238
    (Cornmeal Soufflé)

Galettes de polenta aux raisins • 240
    (Cornmeal Galettes with Raisins)

Gnocchi à la semoule • 241
    (Semolina Gnocchi)

White Dry Beans

Purée de haricots blancs • 243
    (White Bean Puree)

Ragoût haricots blancs • 244
    (White Bean Stew)

Rice

Rizoto maison • 245
    (Risotto My Way)

THIS IS THE TIME OF YEAR when the gardens start coming on hard and fast, when gardeners start to feel that vegetables are taking over their lives . . . that they're not in control anymore; they've planted a glacier out back there and it's moving in on them, their tomatoes are moving in; you get up one morning and the whole kitchen is full of tomatoes lying around on counters. Some of them crept down on the floor, making their way upstairs. Reach for your toothbrush, you might pick up an eggplant. You pick up a newspaper and there'll be 3 zucchini underneath it, come under for the shade or to read the comics, catch a couple zz's. . . . It's the time of year when people take vegetables around to their neighbors' houses late at night, put them on the steps . . .

Summer
TAPE BY GARRISON KEILLOR

IN VALDRÔME, MADAME MAAS is a ninety-eight-year-old gardener whom I have known for thirty years. She is unchanged; still wears her large sun hat, no glasses, a long black dress with the sleeves rolled up. Every morning I see her carrying two large watering cans to her garden (a quarter of a mile from her village house), where she spends mornings and afternoons watering and digging her vegetable garden. It is her life. In winter, she moves in with her children in Montélimar (famous for nougat) and waits for spring. What a relief it must be to go back to Valdrôme and start gardening again!

I admire those die-hard gardeners who live for their gardens; they are the artists of the earth. I remember Nicolas, a young Dutchman who bought a house near us. He planted iceberg lettuce! "But why?" I asked; I never could understand why iceberg lettuce existed in the first place. After eating Nicolas's iceberg lettuce, I shan't ever again say a mean word about iceberg lettuce. It was an unforgettable experience, it was so good!

In the summer, French markets are a joy to shop in. My husband realized we did not need to plant fruit trees or vegetables in our new garden at the château because the markets and our neighbors sell or give us all we need (cheaper, too). We planted herbs and kept the apricot tree for shade, the olive tree because it's Provence, the palm tree because I like it.

In late summer when I start teaching again, I buy thirty pounds of tomatoes for $4.00. Students wonder on Sunday how we are going to cook all of them, but by Friday, they're gone!

Many of the vegetable dishes in this chapter make a whole meal, not just a side dish. I especially think of the variations on a ratatouille. One of my neighbors in Nyons who just bought a house next door came to dinner one night exhausted after working all day long on his house. He ate the whole Ratatouille Terrine (page 225) by himself—he had forgotten to tell me he was a vegetarian!

Artichauts en ragoût

Stew of Baby Artichokes with White Onions and Garlic

IN NYONS, baby artichokes are stewed with onion and garlic in May and June. I serve them as a garnish with Barbecued Pork Shoulder Steaks (page 186) or stuffed in an omelet for lunch. They are also delicious with just a perfect vinaigrette.

SERVES 4

4 to 6 baby artichokes or $1/4$ pound
    Jerusalem artichokes
    (sun chokes),
    peeled and quartered

1 tablespoon olive oil

1 cup quartered white onions

4 large garlic cloves, peeled
    and quartered

1 sprig of fresh thyme

2 wet chicory leaves

$1/2$ teaspoon salt

Freshly ground black pepper

Slice off the artichoke leaves to within $1/4$ inch of the bottom and discard.

Pare the bottom of each artichoke and remove and discard the choke (yields about $1 1/4$ cups bottoms). Brush olive oil on the artichoke bottoms.

In a large braising pan, or nonstick skillet, heat the remaining oil over medium heat. Add the artichokes, onions, and garlic; cook 3 minutes, shaking the pan occasionally.

Add a sprig of fresh thyme and the wet chicory salad leaves and 3 tablespoons water; sprinkle with salt and freshly ground pepper. Cover tightly.

Braise over low to medium heat for 30 minutes, checking occasionally, letting the condensation gathered under the lid of the pan drip on to the vegetables. Add more water if the artichokes are dry.

Taste and correct seasoning.

Topinambours à la provençale

Ragout of Jerusalem Artichokes à la Provençale

WHEN YOU SPEAK about Jerusalem artichokes to a Frenchman who remembers World War II, he will immediately say, *"Quelle horreur!"* Topinambours were about the only vegetable available during the war and this association destroyed the reputation of a good winter vegetable.

In the States, topinambours are either called Jerusalem artichokes or sun chokes.

I buy them when they are firm to the touch. Their knobby quality makes them difficult to peel but that is the most consuming activity of this otherwise very simple recipe. Brush them under running cold water first.

SERVES 4

2 tablespoons olive oil

1^1/$_2$ pounds Jerusalem artichokes, peeled and cut into ^{1}/$_3$-inch cubes (3 cups)

4 large garlic cloves, coarsely chopped

^{1}/$_2$ teaspoon salt

Freshly ground black pepper

In a large nonstick skillet, heat the oil over medium high heat. Sauté the chokes and garlic, stirring, for 1 minute. Sprinkle with salt and freshly ground pepper.

Cover the skillet and braise for 15 to 20 minutes over medium heat, stirring occasionally.

Uncover, raise the heat, and cook for 10 minutes, shaking the pan occasionally, making sure the garlic does not burn.

Serve as is with roasted fowl or meat.

Chartreuse de chou

Cabbage Chartreuse

A CABBAGE *chartreuse* IS a French classic: a molded cabbage dish decorated with slices of zucchini or green beans and carrots. Serve it with roasted fowl for Thanksgiving or Christmas. It's a stunning presentation. It can be prepared ahead of time.

SERVES 8

6 pounds Savoy cabbage(s), stem(s) removed, coarsely chopped

2 or 3 large carrots, peeled and cut into $^{1}/_{16}$-inch-thick slices

1 unpeeled zucchini, cut into $^{1}/_{16}$-inch-thick slices

$1^{1}/_{4}$ teaspoons salt (or more to taste)

Freshly ground black pepper

3 tablespoons olive oil or melted chicken fat

3 onions, minced (3 cups)

3 large garlic cloves, minced

$^{1}/_{8}$ teaspoon grated nutmeg

$1^{1}/_{2}$ cups grated Gruyère cheese

Generously butter a 6-cup soufflé mold and line the bottom with wax paper.

In a very large kettle, boil several quarts of salted water. Add the cabbage and boil for 20 minutes.

Meanwhile, prepare the mold. In a medium pan, boil 2 quarts of water. Add the carrot slices and boil for 5 minutes. Transfer the carrot slices to a bowl of ice water.

Add the zucchini slices to the boiling water and boil for 3 minutes. Transfer to the ice water.

Pat the carrot and zucchini slices dry. Line the sides of the mold with alternating overlapping zucchini and carrot slices. Overlap more vegetables if necessary to eliminate holes. Season them with salt and pepper. Refrigerate the mold for $^{1}/_{2}$ hour to set the vegetables firmly in the mold.

Drain the cabbage. Rinse under cold water. Wrap the cabbage in towels and squeeze both ends of the towels as tightly as possible to extract all the liquid.

continued

In a large nonstick skillet, heat the olive oil over medium heat. Stir in the onions and garlic; cover and braise for 10 minutes.

Add the cabbage, sprinkle with salt, freshly ground pepper, and nutmeg. Stir in the cheese. Set aside to cool for 15 minutes.

Fill the prepared mold with the cabbage mixture. Score the zucchini and carrot slices if they stick out of the rim of the mold and fold over the cabbage. (Can be prepared ahead of time to this step.)

Preheat the oven to 400 degrees.

Line the bottom of a water bath with several layers of newspapers and place the mold on top. Pour boiling water $^2\!/_3$ the way up the mold.

Bake in the oven for 45 minutes. To test for doneness, insert the blade of a knife in the center. It should be barely moist.

Run the blade of a knife around the inside rim of the mold. Unmold on a platter. Discard the wax paper on top. Serve hot.

Carottes braisées aux herbes

Braised Carrots with Fresh Herbs

IF I HAD a vegetable garden, I would plant carrots before any other vegetables! It's a vegetable we buy without thinking of the quality; we're always in search for the perfect tomato, we decry how awful the potatoes are, but we never mention carrots.

What a difference it makes to eat freshly picked carrots instead of the ones we buy in stores. In the States, I am very suspicious of bunches of carrots with their greens attached—they are more expensive than packaged carrots and frequently not as good.

Braised sweet carrots with fresh herbs is an exquisite simple peasant dish; I serve them with Beef Shanks Braised in Onions (page 154).

SERVES 4

1 pound carrots, peeled and cut into sticks

4 tablespoons olive oil

1 teaspoon salt

Freshly ground black pepper

$^1/_3$ cup minced fresh parsley

1 tablespoon minced fresh tarragon

3 garlic cloves, minced

In a large pan with a tight-fitting lid, combine the carrots, oil, salt, and freshly ground pepper.

Cover and simmer over low to medium heat for 15 minutes, occasionally checking.

Sprinkle with the minced parsley, tarragon, and garlic. Cover and braise 5 minutes.

Transfer the carrots to a preheated serving dish. Boil down the carrot juices until syrupy and pour over the carrots. Serve hot.

In the Midi I cook eggplant only in the summer and early fall; a hot climate vegetable, it should never be refrigerated as it becomes mushy. I prefer the medium elongated eggplants, but any size eggplant is good as long as the skin is glossy, the flesh bounces back when pressed with your thumb, and the fruit feels heavy. I never peel eggplants in Nyons, but peel them if you cook them off season. If the eggplants are not picked just ripe, the peels are bitter tasting and tough.

Tian d'aubergines du Comtat Venaissin

Eggplant Gratin from the Vaucluse

I found this recipe in a small booklet published at least fifty years ago on the Comtat Venaissin, the region of the Vaucluse with Avignon its capital. It intrigued me because of its similarity to *Le Risto* (page 21) from Arles, on the other side of the Rhone and south of Avignon. The eggplants here are parboiled instead of deep fried. It's a great favorite of many of my friends who are on diets.

SERVES 4

2 pounds eggplants, cut into
  1/2-inch slices (about 8 cups)

1 tablespoon salt

Freshly ground black pepper

3 cups homemade tomato sauce
  (page 8 or page 10)

1/4 cup grated Parmesan cheese

2 tablespoons olive oil

Preheat the oven to 350 degrees.

Cut the eggplant slices crosswise if very large. Bring a large amount of water to a boil with 2 teaspoons salt. Blanch the eggplants until the slices are soft (5 to 10 minutes). Drain for 10 minutes.

In a 2-quart oiled baking dish, layer half the eggplant slices, season with 1/2 teaspoon salt and freshly ground pepper, pour half the tomato sauce over, and layer the last of the eggplant slices. Season with the remaining salt and pepper and pour the last of the tomato sauce over the eggplants.

Sprinkle cheese and dribble oil on top of the tomato sauce. Bake for 45 minutes, or until the top is light golden brown. Serve hot or at room temperature.

Tian d'aubergines et de poivrons rouges au fromage

Gratin of Eggplants with Red Peppers and Feta Cheese

SERVES 6 TO 8

3 red bell peppers

2 pounds eggplants, cut crosswise on the bias into 1/2-inch-thick slices (about 4 cups)

5 tablespoons olive oil

2 onions, thinly sliced (2 cups)

2 garlic cloves, minced

1 1/2 teaspoons salt

1/2 cup basil leaves

Freshly ground black pepper

1/2 cup crumbled feta cheese or more

Char the peppers on top of the stove or under a broiler. Place them in a sturdy plastic bag and set aside to cool.

Peel the peppers and wash out the burned particles. Quarter and cut each quarter into 2 by 3-inch pieces (this can be done ahead of time); save the juices.

Cut the eggplant slices crosswise if very large. Bring a large amount of water to a boil. Blanch the eggplants until the slices are soft, about 5 to 10 minutes. Drain for 10 minutes.

In a nonstick skillet, heat 2 tablespoons olive oil over medium heat. Cook the onion and garlic for 10 minutes, stirring occasionally.

Preheat the oven to 400 degrees.

Scatter the cooked onion and garlic on the bottom of a 3-quart gratin pan or baking dish.

Starting at a short end of the baking dish, lay down 1 row of tightly overlapping eggplant slices; sprinkle with salt and black pepper. Slip a basil leaf between each slice.

Arrange a row of tightly overlapping peppers next to the eggplant slices. Continue alternating rows of eggplant and peppers down the length of the dish.

Dribble the reserved pepper juice and 3 tablespoons olive oil over the vegetables.

continued

Bake for 45 minutes, checking now and then, pushing down on the vegetables with the back of a large spoon. Baste the eggplant and peppers with the juices at the bottom of the pan.

Sprinkle the crumbled feta over it and bake until the cheese melts and browns, about 10 minutes.

Serve piping hot.

Gratin d'aubergines Uzès

Eggplant Gratin Uzès

UZÈS, A PICTURESQUE small town, is situated near the Pont du Gard and across the Rhone from Avignon. It is interesting to visit these two cities, close to each other but so different.

I ate this gratin for lunch in a small bistro in the Place aux Herbes one very hot summer day without feeling oppressed; the fried eggplants were light and digestible. When the oil is heated to the right temperature (325 degrees), the eggplants do not absorb as much oil as they would if the oil is at a lower temperature. I also tried salting and not salting eggplants before frying; both batches drank up about the same amount of oil.

SERVES 8

3 cups corn oil

3 pounds eggplants, cut lengthwise into $1/4$-inch-thick slices

Flour to dredge the eggplant

2 pounds fresh tomatoes, peeled, seeded, and chopped (4 cups) (see Note, page 9)

$1/2$ cup minced parsley

4 large garlic cloves, minced

2 tablespoons olive oil

$1/2$ teaspoons salt

Freshly ground black pepper

Preheat the oven to 350 degrees.

In a large skillet, heat the corn oil to 325 degrees. Dredge the eggplants one by one in flour and shake off excess. Do this just before frying and do not dredge all the slices at once as they will get gummy while waiting to be fried.

Fry the eggplant slices in several batches, occasionally turning them carefully with tongs. When they are a light golden color, drain on several layers of paper towels.

In a 3-quart baking dish, layer the eggplant slices and tomatoes; sprinkle with parsley, garlic, olive oil, salt, and freshly ground pepper. Repeat, finishing with a layer of eggplant.

continued

Bake for 45 minutes to 1 hour, checking now and then. If the top browns too fast, cover loosely with foil.

Serve hot or at room temperature.

NOTE:

After the tomato season ends, substitute 3 cups of tomato sauce, page 10.

VARIATION

If you dislike frying eggplants, set the broiler on high for 10 minutes.

Brush olive oil on one side of the eggplants and broil 5 inches from the heating element until brown.

Turn the eggplant slices, brush on more olive oil, and broil the other side.

Sauté d'aubergines et de poivrons à l'ail

Pan-Fried Eggplants and Peppers with Garlic

ONE SUMMER, MY friend Aline Boschi and I drove to Anduze on the west side of the Rhone to shop for pottery, a favorite summer activity. Aline is an excellent cook, and what do two cooks do while driving? They exchange recipes! This is Aline's recipe; I love the pottery, but the recipe is the best reward of the trip.

I serve this cold as an appetizer on top of toasts rubbed with garlic or hot on top of rice for a vegetable course.

Cut the eggplants and peppers into thick french-fry shapes, about 3 inches long and ½ inch thick. Choose small elongated eggplants, which are easier to cut in french-fry shape.

SERVES 10 AS AN APPETIZER; 6 AS A VEGETABLE COURSE

½ cup olive oil

1½ pounds eggplants, cut into large french-fry shapes (8 cups)

1 pound red peppers, cut into large french-fry shapes (4 cups)

1 teaspoon salt

2 large garlic cloves

In each of 2 large nonstick skillets, heat ¼ cup olive oil. When the oil is almost smoking, stir fry the eggplants and the peppers, each in its own skillet, about 5 minutes.

Lower the heat and cover each skillet. Braise for 5 minutes, stirring occasionally.

Uncover and cook 15 minutes, stirring or shaking the pans.

Sprinkle with the salt and garlic, stir and cook for 2 minutes.

Purée de fèves

Fava Bean Puree

THIS IS MY favorite May and June vegetable puree with roasted fowl or meat. My students react with a variety of attitudes toward fava or fava beans: The lazy ones can't be bothered to shell the beans and to force them through a kitchen sieve; others are so crazy about the result that they don't care about the amount of work. Substitute White Bean Puree (page 243) if you think you belong in the first group.

Be sure to buy plump green pods; avoid yellowish green pods, which are over the hill and bitter when cooked.

SERVES 6

6 pounds fava beans (6 cups shelled)

1/4 cup olive oil

1 large fresh tomato, chopped or 1 cup chopped cherry tomatoes

3 garlic cloves, chopped coarsely

1 1/2 teaspoons salt

Freshly ground black pepper

In a large pan, cover the beans with water and bring to a boil. Drain and pat dry with paper towels. Wet beans will spatter in the hot oil of the next step.

In a large skillet, heat the olive oil over medium high heat. Sauté the beans, tomato, and garlic for 2 minutes.

Add 4 cups water. Sprinkle with 1 1/2 teaspoons salt and freshly ground pepper. Cover tightly and cook until the fava beans are tender, about 20 to 30 minutes, stirring occasionally.

Drain the beans and reserve the bean liquid.

Process the beans for 1 minute with 1/4 to 1/2 cup of bean liquid. Reserve remaining liquid. Force through a kitchen sieve, pushing on the beans with the back of a spoon; discard the skins. Taste and correct seasoning (can be prepared ahead to this point).

Reheat the puree, whisking in 1/4 cup or more of any remaining bean liquid or water. Cover and simmer for 10 minutes, or until hot. Be careful not to burn the puree.

FENNEL SHOWS UP in markets in early fall, which is the best time to cook it. In late winter, fennel loses its anise aroma. Once in one of my classes, I rhapsodized on the aroma of fennel, which was greeted with blank looks by the student who was cleaning it. It had no scent left. I had left it too long in the refrigerator. Now when I buy it, I sniff it very carefully and I make sure to cook it as soon as possible after buying it.

Fenouil rôti

Roasted Fennel

SERVES 4

3 small fennel bulbs

1/4 cup olive oil

1 teaspoon salt (more or less)

Freshly ground black pepper

1/2 cup grated Gruyère cheese

Preheat the oven to 425 degrees.

Discard the stalks if they have not been removed beforehand in the market. Cut the fennel bulbs in half lengthwise; cut each half into thirds.

In a large saucepan, cover the fennel with salted water. Bring to a boil, cover, and cook for 15 minutes. Drain.

Pour olive oil into a 3-quart gratin dish. Turn the fennel over and over in the oil to coat it. Sprinkle with the salt and freshly ground pepper.

Roast the fennel on the middle shelf of the oven for 30 minutes, turning the fennel over occasionally.

Sprinkle with the cheese and serve piping hot.

Fondue de fenouil

Fondue of Fennel

SERVES 6

3 pounds fennel bulbs

2 tablespoons olive oil

1 teaspoon salt

Freshly ground black pepper

Slice the fennel bulbs into ¼-inch slices; cut each slice in $1/4$-inch strips (yields 9 cups).

Heat the oil in a 6-quart dutch oven. Sauté the fennel for 2 minutes. Sprinkle with salt and freshly ground pepper. Cover and cook the fennel over medium heat until tender, stirring from time to time, about 45 minutes.

Uncover and boil away the liquid remaining in the pan.

In a food processor, coarsely puree the fennel. Taste and correct seasoning.

Reheat and serve immediately.

THE FOLLOWING RECIPES are for young, sweet peas. I try to shell peas when someone is in the kitchen to help or at least keep me company. When I was a child, I was always put in charge of shelling. My technique was to find an old newspaper with the comics; today I watch TV reruns—*Hawaï, Police d'État* (*Hawaii Five-O*) is my favorite!

After shelling the peas, there is no work. Cook them just before serving; reheated peas shrivel.

Petits pois à la française

Peas Braised with Salad Greens

SERVES 6

6 cups shelled peas (about 5 pounds in the pod)

3 salad leaves, shredded

1 teaspoon salt

1 tablespoon sugar

Combine the peas, salad leaves, salt, sugar, and 1 cup water in a stainless steel pan. Cover tightly and cook over low heat for 10 minutes or until the peas are cooked.

Purée de petits pois à l'ail

Green Pea Puree with Garlic

SERVES 6

6 cups shelled peas (about 5
    pounds in the pod)

3 sprigs of fresh thyme

1/4 cup olive oil

6 garlic cloves, unpeeled

2 teaspoons salt

Freshly ground black pepper

In a large pan, cover the peas with 5 cups water, fresh thyme, oil, and garlic. Sprinkle with salt and pepper. When the water boils, cook 10 to 15 minutes until the peas are tender.

Drain the peas (reserve the cooking liquid). Peel the garlic cloves.

Boil down the cooking liquid for 5 minutes, to 1 1/2 cups.

Puree the peas and garlic in batches with 1 cup cooking liquid. Taste and correct seasoning.

Cover and reheat in a water bath to avoid burning the bottom of the puree before serving. (Add more cooking liquid to the puree if necessary.)

HUNTING FOR WILD MUSHROOMS is very serious business for amateur mycologists the world over. In Nyons, my neighbors start talking about their forthcoming mushrooming excursions at least a month before there are any mushrooms to harvest. The mushroom-hunting fever mounts toward the middle of September when the first autumnal rains come and the talk turns anticipatory. The first serious gathering is in October.

The hunters wait for the perfect moment: a bright day after a long rain. All go to bed early preparing for an early wake-up to pick mushrooms and to spy on one another.

In *Leaving Home,* Garrison Keillor's collection of Lake Wobegon stories, he characterizes mushroom hunters: "Morel mushrooms are a great delicacy. They are found in the wild by people who walk fifteen miles through the woods to get ten of them and then never tell the location to a soul, not even on their deathbeds to a priest." Keillor was perhaps kidding, but it happened to my friend André who was near death. His son-in-law wanted to know where his secret morel patch was, but André refused to tell. Fortunately for André, he recuperated and still is the only one who knows of that morel patch.

Confit de pommes de terre et barigoules

Confit of Potatoes with Wild Mushrooms

WHEN I WAS cooking potatoes every day and researching my book *A Passion for Potatoes,* I found *Pommes de terre à la barigoule* in *La Cuisinière républicaine,* an eighteenth-century cookbook published during the French Revolution. A *barigoule* is a morel or other wild mushroom but in the culinary term "*à la barigoule,*" which means braising, morels are not included.

I decided to add morels to the potato confit; it's good. I serve it with the Ragout of Jerusalem Artichokes à la Provençale (page 196).

SERVES 6

continued

½ ounce dried morels

3 tablespoons olive oil

2 pounds fingerling potatoes or
   creamers, peeled

1½ teaspoons salt

Freshly ground black pepper

About ½ cup 1-Hour Rich Broth
   (page 12)

In a medium bowl, soak the morels in 1 cup warm water for ½ hour.

Line a strainer with a double thickness of cheesecloth and drain the morels over a bowl. Reserve the morel liquid for another preparation, such as adding it to a stew, basting a roast, or combining with a tomato or other pasta sauce.

Wash the morels under cold running water to remove any sand left on the stems.

In a large skillet, heat the oil over high heat. Stir fry the potatoes for 5 minutes or until the potatoes are lightly golden brown.

Discard the fat and add the morels. Sprinkle with salt and freshly ground pepper. Pour ½ cup broth over the potatoes and morels; lower the heat, and cook, partially covered, until the broth is totally evaporated, about 20 minutes.

If the potatoes are not tender at that point, add ¼ cup more broth and cook, partially covered, until tender, about 5 minutes, depending on the variety of potato.

Serve immediately.

Gratin d'oignons et morilles

Onion and Morel Gratin

WHEN ONIONS ARE cooked, they have a sweet and delicate flavor. I bake the onions in a béchamel sauce with morels; it's the vegetable par excellence to accompany such strong-flavored meat as lamb.

To peel onions, I put on my swimmer's goggles. It does the trick, no tears. I saw it in a French cops-and-robbers film, *Diva*, where the "hero" is in the kitchen peeling and cutting onions with goggles on. I tried it and it works.

SERVES 6 TO 8

1 ounce dried morels	$1^1/_2$ cups scalded milk
3 pounds large onions, peeled and cut into $^1/_8$-inch rings	2 teaspoons salt
3 tablespoons plus 1 teaspoon olive oil	Freshly ground black pepper
	1 to $1^1/_2$ cups grated Gruyère cheese
3 tablespoons flour	

In a medium bowl, soak the morels in $1^1/_2$ cups warm water for $^1/_2$ hour.

Line a strainer with a double thickness of cheesecloth and drain the morels over a bowl. Set the morels aside. Boil the morel liquid down to $^3/_4$ cup. Set aside.

In a large pot, bring several quarts of salted water to a boil. Add the onion rings and count 15 minutes after the water reboils. Drain. Yields 9 to 10 cups.

In a sturdy saucepan, heat 3 tablespoons olive oil. Add the flour and whisk until smooth. Whisk in the hot milk and the morel liquid. Sprinkle with 1 teaspoon salt and freshly ground pepper. Cook over low-medium heat for 20 minutes, whisking now and then.

Preheat the oven to 400 degrees.

Wash the morels under cold running water to remove any sand left on the stems; chop them coarsely.

continued

Drizzle 1 teaspoon oil on the bottom of a 3-quart baking pan and add the onions and morels; sprinkle with 1 teaspoon salt and freshly ground pepper. Pour the sauce over it and sprinkle with Gruyère.

Bake 30 minutes or until brown on top. Set aside pan 10 minutes before serving.

VARIATION

Gratin d'endives et de morilles

BELGIAN ENDIVES AND MOREL GRATIN

IN WINTER I sometimes substitute Belgian endives for the onions.

SERVES 6

2 pounds Belgian endives

**1 tablespoon freshly squeezed
   lemon juice**

Remove the cone-shaped bitter center of the endives' stems.

In a large pot, bring several quarts of salted water to a boil. Add the lemon juice.

Boil the endives for 10 minutes or until almost tender.

Drain the endives and gently squeeze out any remaining water.

Split the endives in half lengthwise. Put them in an oiled baking pan as in the above recipe and proceed with the morels and béchamel sauce as above.

Girolles braisées à l'ail et aux échalotes

Braised Chanterelles with Garlic and Shallots

MY FIRST WILD mushroom hunt was in the rainy summer of 1977 in Valdrôme. Our neighbor Bébert showed us how to pick small *girolles* called *craterelles,* delicate chanterelles hiding in the moss. It was exhilarating to find hundreds of them and so close to home. I quickly sauté the mushrooms with shallots and stuff omelets with them. I also throw them into a tossed salad of greens and tomatoes.

SERVES 4

$^1/_2$ pound chanterelles

2 tablespoons olive oil

4 large shallots, thinly sliced

$^1/_2$ teaspoon salt

Freshly ground black pepper

With a damp paper towel, clean the mushrooms. Trim the stems if need be.

In a large skillet, heat the oil over medium high heat; sauté the chanterelles and shallots, salt, and pepper for 2 minutes.

Cover and braise over low heat for 10 minutes.

Uncover, raise the heat, and stir fry until the mushroom liquid has evaporated. Correct seasoning.

Les Cèpes farcies

Stuffed Porcini Caps

IN THE FALL, several vendors in my weekly market in Nyons display an enticing variety of wild mushrooms on long narrow tables. I choose among *cèpes* (porcini), chanterelles, and others.

SERVES 6

1 pound *cèpes* (porcini), caps and stems separated

4 tablespoons olive oil

1 tablespoon minced fresh thyme leaves

1 teaspoon salt

1 tablespoon minced garlic

$1/2$ cup minced parsley

1 tablespoon minced fresh tarragon

1 large slice bread soaked in $1/3$ cup milk

Freshly ground black pepper

Place the mushroom caps in a strainer and quickly rinse them under running cold water. Pat dry with paper towels.

In a mixing bowl, combine 3 tablespoons oil, thyme, and $1/2$ teaspoon salt. Toss in the mushroom caps and set aside for 1 hour.

Scrape off the dirt and trim the ends of the stems. Mince the stems; depending on their thickness, you will have about $2^1/2$ cups.

In a large nonstick skillet, heat 2 teaspoons oil over medium high heat. Stir fry the garlic and remaining herbs for 1 minute.

Mix in the minced mushroom stems sprinkled with $1/2$ teaspoon salt and black pepper. Cook over medium heat for 3 minutes or until the liquid rendered by the stems evaporates.

Add the bread soaked in milk and mix until smooth. Set aside.

In a clean skillet, place the mushroom caps, top side down, and spread the filling on the underside of the mushroom caps. Pour 2 tablespoons water on the bottom of the skillet; drizzle 1 teaspoon oil over the stuffing. Cover tightly and braise over medium heat for 10 minutes or until the caps are cooked through.

Serve hot.

Stuffed Portobello Mushrooms

The stems of the portobello mushrooms are not as meaty as the *cèpes;* adjust the amount of bread and milk. When I tested the recipe with portobellos, I used only $1/2$ cup bread soaked in $1/4$ cup milk for $1^1/2$ cups minced stems but kept the same amount of herbs and garlic.

In August, most Provençal villages have their annual *brocante*, a flea market that attracts regional dealers of antique furniture, linens, hardware, and old books. I go to as many as I can to find old cookbooks. I sometimes find wonderful old recipes like Scalloped Potatoes with Cheese (page 220) and the following Potato Puffs.

Croquettes de pommes de terre

Potato Puffs

THE PUFFS ARE made with all-purpose potatoes mashed with flour. Just like Italian gnocchi, but deep fried instead of poached, the mashed potatoes puff in the hot oil.

I serve the puffs as an appetizer or for a Sunday supper with a large salad of greens, tomatoes, and olives. I also dip them in sugar for dessert fritters.

MAKES TWENTY-FOUR 2 ^{1}/$_2$-INCH PUFFS; SERVES 6
FOR SUPPER OR DESSERT

1 pound all-purpose potatoes
  (Kennebec, Mona Lisa,
  Superior, Yukon Gold), peeled
  and quartered (3 cups)

^{1}/$_2$ cup flour

1 quart corn oil

Salt or sugar

In a large pan, cover the potatoes with salted water and cook until very tender; depending on the potatoes, it takes about 20 to 30 minutes.

Drain and quickly mash the potatoes while they are still hot with a ricer or in a food mill. (Yields 2 cups mashed potatoes.)

In a large mixing bowl, combine the mashed potatoes and flour until smooth.

On a floured surface and with a floured rolling pin, gently roll the dough to about a 12-inch circle, flouring the pin once in a while to avoid sticking.

Stamp out two ^{1}/$_2$-inch circles with a glass or cookie cutter. Place the potato circles on a clean towel. Roll out the leftovers and stamp out more circles.

Heat the oil to 325 degrees and fry the puffs in 3 batches until they are puffy and golden brown.

Line a serving platter with a clean tea towel and transfer the puffs to the towel. Sprinkle with salt or dip them in lots of sugar if you serve them for dessert.

Gratin de pommes de terre au fromage

Scalloped Potatoes with Cheese

SERVES 8

3 pounds all-purpose potatoes (Yukon Gold, Kennebec, etc.), cut into $1/8$- to $1/6$-inch-thick slices (about 9 cups)

$1^{1}/_{4}$ cups grated Gruyère cheese

3 tablespoons all-purpose flour

2 tablespoons unsalted butter

$1^{1}/_{2}$ teaspoons salt

Freshly ground black pepper

4 cups Light Broth (page 11)

Preheat the oven to 375 degrees.

In a large bowl, toss the potatoes with $1/2$ cup Gruyère cheese and the flour.

Generously grease a 3-quart gratin or baking dish. Make 3 layers of potatoes, sprinkling cheese, butter, salt, and pepper between each layer and on top.

Pour the broth over the top and bake for $1^{1}/_{2}$ hours or until the potatoes are tender and golden brown on top. Serve piping hot.

Purée de pommes de terre au fromage de chèvre

Mashed Potatoes with Goat Cheese

IN NYONS, I buy fresh goat cheese made the evening before; in the States, I substitute Bucheron goat cheese and milk.

For the best mashed potatoes, choose potatoes of uniform size. I prefer small ones, which cook faster and more evenly. Cook them in their jackets, drain and peel immediately—the most important step (wear gloves to avoid burning yourself). If the potatoes cool before they are mashed, they will turn gluey. For a large quantity of potatoes, I mash them in a food mill or in a heavy-duty mixer.

SERVES 8

4 pounds russet potatoes

1/2 pound imported Bucheron
   goat cheese

1 1/2 to 2 cups milk

4 tablespoons olive oil

2 1/2 teaspoons salt

Freshly ground black pepper

In a large pan, cover the potatoes with a generous amount of cold water and bring to a boil. Cook until tender (about 25 minutes).

Scrape off the rind of the cheese. Process in the food processor with 1 cup (or more) milk until creamy.

Drain the potatoes; quickly peel and mash while still hot (the most important step in the creation of perfect mashed potatoes).

Whisk in the olive oil, salt, and freshly ground pepper.

Reheat and gradually beat in the cheese mixture. Whisk in more milk if necessary. Taste and correct seasoning. Serve hot.

Purée de pommes de terre grand-mère

Old-Fashioned Mashed Potatoes

I EAT POTATOES almost every day. For special occasions, I make old-fashioned mashed potatoes with butter and milk. What a treat.

For the best results, mash the potatoes as soon as they are cooked otherwise the potatoes become gluey; cook the potatoes just before dinner.

SERVES 6

3 pounds russet or Yukon Gold potatoes, peeled and cut into 2-inch cubes (8 cups)

6 tablespoons unsalted butter

1¹/₂ to 2 cups scalded milk

2 teaspoons salt

Freshly ground black pepper

In a large pan, cover the potatoes with cold salted water. Bring to a boil, partially cover, and cook for 20 minutes, or until the potatoes are tender

Drain the potatoes. Add the butter to the cooking pot and over low heat mash the potatoes in the pot through a vegetable mill or ricer, gradually adding 1 cup scalded milk.

Whisk in more milk and sprinkle with salt and pepper. Whisk for several minutes, tasting and adding more seasoning and more milk if need be. Serve right away.

VARIATION

For guests I prepare old-fashioned mashed potatoes, but for my family I substitute 1 percent fat milk, and for butter, I whisk in 2 large minced garlic cloves and ¹/₃ cup minced fresh parsley.

Gratin de coucourdon

Pumpkin Gratin

I HAD FRIENDS in Pernes-les-Fontaines, a village east of Avignon in the Vaucluse, who always made this dish in the fall. Here I offer their 2 versions, with and without a béchamel.

SERVES 4

3 tablespoons olive oil

4 cups diced pumpkin flesh
   (3–pound pumpkin)

1 tablespoon minced garlic

1 teaspoon salt

Freshly ground black pepper

FOR THE BÉCHAMEL

2 tablespoons olive oil

2 tablespoons flour

1 1/2 cups scalded milk

1/4 cup minced onions

1/2 teaspoon salt

1/8 teaspoon grated nutmeg

2 eggs

1/4 cup homemade bread crumbs

In a large nonstick skillet, heat 3 tablespoons olive oil over medium high heat. Sauté the pumpkin meat for 3 minutes. Lower the heat, add the garlic, sprinkle with 1 teaspoon salt and freshly ground pepper. Cover and cook over low heat until the pumpkin is very soft, about 30 minutes.

Preheat the oven to 325 degrees. Oil a 4-cup gratin dish.

In a heavy-bottomed saucepan, heat the remaining 2 tablespoons oil over medium heat. Whisk in the flour, add the hot milk, and whisk until smooth. Add the onions, sprinkle with 1/2 teaspoon salt and nutmeg. Cook for 20 minutes over low heat, stirring occasionally. Add more milk if the béchamel gets too thick—it should have the consistency of thick buttermilk.

Combine the pumpkin, béchamel, and eggs. Pour into the gratin dish, sprinkle with bread crumbs, and bake for 1 hour, or until the top is golden.

continued

Gratin léger de coucourdon

LIGHT PUMPKIN GRATIN

SERVES 4

$^1/_2$ cup bread crumbs

1 teaspoon minced garlic

$^1/_4$ cup minced parsley

1 heaping teaspoon salt

Freshly ground black pepper

4 cups diced pumpkin flesh
   (3-pound pumpkin)

$1^1/_4$ cups low fat milk

2 teaspoons olive oil

Preheat the oven to 350 degrees. Oil a 4-cup gratin dish.

Combine the bread crumbs, garlic, parsley, salt, and pepper. Dredge the pumpkin pieces in the mixture.

Place in the baking dish; pour over the milk and dribble on the olive oil. Bake for 1 to 1½ hours or until golden. Serve hot.

Around a Ratatouille

I CAN'T WAIT for late June when eggplants, tomatoes, and peppers are just turning up in my weekly market and I cook the first ratatouille of the year. There are many ways to prepare a good ratatouille, and each cook likes her or his best. Some cooks broil the vegetables separately to give the ratatouille a smoky flavor, others roast the vegetables in the oven, and others sauté them. But we all agree not to cook the vegetables into a mush.

Ratatouille en terrine

Ratatouille Terrine

THIS RUSTIC RATATOUILLE of sautéed vegetables is baked in a tian, a deep dish of provençal pottery. In New York, I bake it in a dutch oven. Serve it hot or cold for a first course, a vegetable course, or a vegeterian dinner.

SERVES 8 FOR A FIRST OR VEGETABLE COURSE; 4 FOR A MAIN COURSE

½ cup olive oil or more

2 onions, thinly sliced (2 cups)

1 cup grated Gruyère cheese

1 pound unpeeled zucchini, cut in ¼-inch slices (4 cups)

½ cup basil leaves

2 teaspoons salt

Large pinch of cayenne

2 large red bell peppers, cut into ¼-inch round slices, core and seeds removed (4 cups)

1 pound eggplant, cut into ¼-inch slices (4 cups)

2 pounds unpeeled fresh tomatoes, cut into ¼-inch slices (4 cups)

1 tablespoon fresh thyme leaves

1 cup coarse bread crumbs or more

Preheat oven to 350 degrees.

In a large nonstick skillet, heat 1 tablespoon olive oil over medium heat. Cook the onions for 5 minutes, stirring occasionally.

continued

Transfer the onions to a 6-quart dutch oven. Sprinkle ¼ cup cheese over the onions.

In the same skillet, heat 2 more tablespoons olive oil and sauté the zucchini in batches for 5 minutes, adding more oil if necessary and continually stirring.

Layer the zucchini slices and several basil leaves over the cheese. Sprinkle with ½ teaspoon salt and a light pinch of cayenne.

In the same skillet, heat 1 tablespoon olive oil and sauté the peppers for 5 minutes.

Layer the peppers and several basil leaves over the zucchini. Sprinkle with ½ teaspoon salt and a light pinch of cayenne.

In the same skillet, heat 2 tablespoons oil and sauté as many eggplant slices as will fit in a single layer for 5 minutes. Repeat, adding more oil if necessary, making sure to heat it before adding a new batch of eggplant slices.

Layer the eggplant slices and more basil leaves on top of the peppers. Sprinkle with ½ teaspoon salt and a light pinch of cayenne.

In the same skillet, heat 2 tablespoons oil and sauté the tomato slices in batches for 2 minutes.

Layer the tomatoes and the last basil leaves on top of the eggplant. Sprinkle with ½ teaspoon salt and a light pinch of cayenne.

Sprinkle with the remaining cheese, the thyme leaves, and the bread crumbs, covering the tomatoes.

Cover with foil or a lid and bake for 30 minutes on the middle shelf of the oven. After 30 minutes, uncover and bake for 30 minutes more to brown the top.

Serve hot, warm, or cold.

Ratatouille niçoise au bacon et aux pâtes fraîches

Ratatouille from Nice with Bacon and Fresh Pasta

THE PREPARATION OF the vegetables before cooking is the only time-consuming aspect of this recipe. Have all the ingredients prepared before you start to cook.

SERVES 8

6 ounces very lean bacon

1 pound red bell peppers (about 2 large peppers)

$3/4$ pound zucchini

$1^1/2$ pounds juicy fresh tomatoes

1 pound eggplants

$1/4$ cup olive oil

$1^1/2$ cups coarsely chopped onions

1 tablespoon minced garlic

1 teaspoon salt

Freshly ground black pepper

$1^1/2$ pounds Fresh Egg Pasta, cut into fettucine (page 31)

Dice the bacon and all the vegetables into $1/4$-inch cubes. You should have about 1 cup bacon, 3 cups red bell peppers, $2^1/2$ cups zucchini, $4^1/2$ cups peeled and seeded tomatoes (see Note, page 9), and 4 cups eggplants.

In a 6-quart dutch oven, heat 1 tablespoon olive oil over medium high heat. Add the bacon and cook, occasionally stirring until lightly brown, about 10 minutes.

Stir in the peppers, onions, and garlic. Cover and cook over medium low heat, stirring occasionally until the vegetables are soft, about 30 minutes.

Stir in the zucchini, cover, and cook another 10 minutes, until just soft.

Add the eggplants and tomatoes. Mix in the remaining oil, sprinkle with salt and freshly ground pepper. Cover and cook over medium low heat until the eggplants are soft, about 20 minutes.

With a large slotted spoon transfer the vegetables to a large strainer set over a bowl. Boil the vegetable liquid that drains from the vegetables until slightly syrupy, about 15 minutes. Yields about $1^1/2$ cups vegetable sauce.

continued

Return the vegetables to the sauce in the dutch oven and stir. Taste and correct seasoning.

Bring a large pot of salted water to a boil over high heat. Add the fettucine and cook until al dente. Drain.

In a large serving bowl, toss the fettucine with the ratatouille and serve immediately.

VARIATION

Ratatouille au fromage de chèvre

RATATOUILLE AND GOAT CHEESE

**¼ pound imported Bucheron goat
cheese, rind removed, or other
soft goat cheese**

Omit the bacon, adding 2 extra tablespoons olive oil to sauté the peppers, onions, and garlic.

Crumble the goat cheese over the pasta and the ratatouille and toss.

Ratatouille en 15 minutes

15-Minute Ratatouille

WHEN I HAVE a last-minute dinner guest during eggplant and tomato season, I make this very fast ratatouille with onion, garlic, eggplants, and tomatoes. Remember, this is quick because it serves only 2 or 3 people. As soon as you double or triple the recipe, the result will be different and it will take longer.

SERVES 2 TO 3

1/4 cup olive oil

2 medium onions, coarsely chopped (2 cups)

4 large garlic cloves, coarsely chopped

1 pound fresh tomatoes, chopped (3 cups)

1 teaspoon sugar

2 teaspoons salt

Pinch of cayenne

1/4 cup tightly packed chopped basil leaves

1/2 pound eggplant, cut into 1/4-inch cubes (3 cups)

In a large nonstick pan or skillet, heat the oil. Add the onions and garlic and cook for 5 minutes, stirring occasionally.

Add the tomatoes, sugar, salt, cayenne, and basil. Stir and cover. Cook for 5 minutes. Lift the lid and let the water condensation fall back into the tomatoes.

Stir the eggplant into the tomatoes. Cover and cook for 5 minutes or until the eggplant is soft.

Épinards aux oeufs durs et aux croûtons

Spinach in a Béchamel with Hard-Boiled Eggs and Croutons

GEORGETTE ODDON, one of my best sources for good country food, cooks spinach to please her young granddaughter. This traditional French preparation pleased me as a child, too.

Be sure to squeeze the boiled spinach very dry; otherwise the result will give you a so-so dish instead of a good one.

SERVES 6

6 pounds spinach, thoroughly washed and stems removed or 3 pounds young tender spinach

2 teaspoons salt

1 1/2 tablespoons olive oil

1 1/2 tablespoons flour

1 1/2 cups scalded milk

Pinch of grated nutmeg

2 hard-boiled eggs (for garnish)

Croutons (page 39) (about 1 cup) (for garnish)

In a large kettle, bring several quarts of water to a boil. Plunge in the spinach, bring the water back to a boil, and sprinkle with 1 1/2 teaspoons salt. Count 2 minutes from the time the water boils again.

Drain and rinse the spinach under cold water. Squeeze very dry and finely chop the spinach. You should have 4 cups chopped spinach.

In a medium saucepan, heat the oil and whisk in the flour until smooth. Add half the hot milk and whisk briskly.

Cook over low to medium heat for 20 minutes, gradually whisking in the remaining milk. Sprinkle with 1/2 teaspoon salt and the nutmeg.

Combine the spinach and the béchamel in a preheated serving dish. Decorate with sliced hard-boiled eggs and croutons. Serve hot.

Tétragone à l'ail

Sautéed New Zealand Spinach with Garlic

THIS TYPE OF spinach originated in New Zealand and was brought to Europe by Captain Cook. I find it in France from mid-June to mid-July and in July at New York's farmers' markets. Substitute spinach or Swiss chard if you can't find it.

SERVES 6

3 pounds New Zealand spinach or spinach leaves, washed and dried

4 large garlic cloves, peeled and cut lengthwise into 1/8-inch-thick slices

3 tablespoons olive oil

1 teaspoon salt

Freshly ground black pepper

Cook the spinach and garlic in 3 batches. In a large nonstick skillet, heat 1 tablespoon oil. Add a third of the garlic and spinach; stir in the oil for 2 to 3 minutes. Sprinkle with 1/4 teaspoon salt.

When the spinach is wilted and most of the liquid is evaporated transfer it to a preheated dish and stir fry the next 2 batches.

Season with the remaining salt and freshly ground pepper. Serve immediately.

Tomates provençales légères

Tomatoes à la Provençale

EVERY COOK I know has a way to cook tomatoes à la Provençale. I like Jeanine's method, which I offer here.

Choose ripe but firm tomatoes, and make your own bread crumbs.

SERVES 4

4 medium firm fresh tomatoes, sliced horizontally in half

1 teaspoon salt

Freshly ground black pepper

2 tablespoons minced garlic

⅓ cup minced parsley

2 tablespoons fine homemade bread crumbs

3 tablespoons olive oil

Sprinkle the tomato halves with salt and pepper.

Layer the garlic, parsley, and bread crumbs on the tomatoes.

In a large nonstick skillet, heat the oil. Add the tomato halves, cut side up.

Turn the heat on high for 2 minutes. Lower the heat to medium and cook the tomatoes for 15 minutes.

Cover and braise for 20 minutes.

Serve hot around a roast or with broiled chops.

Tian de tomates

Tomato Gratin

I MAKE THIS dish when plum tomatoes are at their peak. With "Styrofoam" tomatoes, the gratin tastes blah and isn't worth making.

SERVES 6

1 pound potatoes, peeled and
 sliced $^1/_{16}$ inch thick (2 cups)

4 tablespoons olive oil

1 pound onions, peeled and sliced
 (4 cups)

3 pounds fresh plum tomatoes,
 peeled and sliced $^1/_4$ inch
 thick (8 cups) (see Note,
 page 9)

$^1/_4$ cup shredded basil leaves

$^3/_4$ cup grated Gruyère cheese

$1^1/_2$ teaspoons salt

Freshly ground black pepper

Cover the potatoes with $1^1/_2$ cups water. Bring to a boil and cook for 5 minutes. Drain and reserve.

In a large nonstick skillet, heat 1 tablespoon olive oil and stir in the onions. Add 2 tablespoons water. Cover and cook 10 minutes or until the onions are wilted. Transfer to a plate and set aside.

In the same large skillet, heat the remaining oil and sauté the tomato slices in batches, 3 minutes for each batch.

Preheat the oven to 350 degrees.

Arrange half the tomatoes in the bottom of a 3-quart baking dish. Scatter half the onions on top of the tomatoes and sprinkle with half the shredded basil and $^1/_3$ cup cheese. Sprinkle with $^1/_2$ teaspoon salt and freshly ground pepper.

Layer on the potatoes and sprinkle with $^1/_2$ teaspoon salt and pepper. Scatter the remaining onions, basil, and $^1/_3$ cup cheese. Top with the remaining slices of tomatoes. Sprinkle with the last of the cheese, salt, and pepper.

Bake for 45 minutes or until golden brown. Serve piping hot.

Petits navets nouveaux sautés

Sautéed Young Turnips

I COOK TURNIPS only in early fall when the turnips are firm and sweet.

SERVES 6

2 pounds turnips, cut into eighths

2 tablespoons olive oil

1 teaspoon fresh thyme leaves

1 teaspoon salt

Freshly ground black pepper

In a large pan, cover the turnips with salted water and bring to a boil.

Boil the turnips for 10 minutes. Drain over a mixing bowl. Reserve the liquid for a soup or for basting a roast. It can be prepared ahead up until this point.

In a large nonstick skillet, heat 2 tablespoons oil. Toss in turnips and thyme. Sprinkle with 1 teaspoon salt and freshly ground pepper.

Cook over low heat for 15 minutes or until tender, occasionally shaking the pan. Serve right away.

Courgettes poêlées, à l'ail et au gruyère

Pan-Fried Zucchini with Garlic and Gruyère

SERVES 6

4 tablespoons olive oil

6 small zucchini (about 1½ pounds), brushed clean and split in half lengthwise

4 garlic cloves, minced

2 teaspoons fresh thyme leaves

1 teaspoon salt

Freshly ground black pepper

½ cup freshly grated Gruyère cheese

In a large nonstick skillet, heat 2 tablespoons oil to the smoking point. Sauté half of the zucchini for 5 minutes or until they are lightly golden brown; transfer to a plate.

Heat 2 more tablespoons oil in the skillet. Sauté the remaining zucchini. Transfer the zucchini in the plate back to the skillet and sprinkle with garlic, thyme, salt, and pepper. Cover the skillet and braise over low heat for 5 minutes, turning the zucchini 2 or 3 times.

Sprinkle the cheese on the cut side of the zucchini. Cover the skillet and cook over low heat for 2 minutes, just enough time to melt the cheese. Serve immediately.

Gratin de courgettes épicées

Spicy Zucchini Gratin

THIS IS A pretty dish, suited for large parties. It can be assembled several hours before baking, but as soon as it comes out of the oven, it must be served.

SERVES 8 TO 10

3 garlic cloves, minced

4 eggs

²/₃ cup sour cream

¹/₂ cup milk

Pinch of curry powder

Pinch of cumin

Pinch of grated nutmeg

Pinch of cayenne

1 teaspoon salt

¹/₂ teaspoon freshly ground black
  pepper

2 teaspoons fresh thyme leaves

4 small zucchini, cut into ¹/₈-inch-
  thick slices (4 cups)

10 fresh plum tomatoes, peeled and
  sliced ¹/₈ inch thick (4 cups)
  (see Note, page 9)

Preheat the oven to 400 degrees. Oil a 15 by 12-inch broiler pan.

Scatter the minced garlic over the bottom of the pan.

In a large mixing bowl, combine the eggs, sour cream, milk, curry powder, cumin, nutmeg, cayenne, ¹/₂ teaspoon salt, ¹/₂ teaspoon freshly ground pepper, and 1 teaspoon thyme leaves.

In a large mixing bowl, toss the zucchini and tomatoes with remaining thyme leaves and salt.

Alternate rows of zucchini and tomato slices in the pan.

Bake the vegetables for 5 minutes.

Pour the egg-cream mixture over the vegetables and bake for 20 minutes or until the custard is set but not dry.

Serve immediately.

Gratin de courgettes aux oignons

Squash and Onion Gratin

EVERY YEAR, I tell Georgette Oddon, my friend and neighbor, to plant fewer zucchini. She can't help herself—every year the zucchini patch grows larger and larger. French thrift is my nature, so I had to devise ways to cook all those oversized zucchini—I just could not throw them out. I suspect that all my gardening friends give away their excess vegetables to alleviate the burden of guilt that goes with throwing out food!

SERVES 6 TO 8

5 pounds zucchini or yellow squash, peeled and cut into 1/2-inch cubes (18 cups)

4 large onions, thinly sliced (6 cups)

1 cup fresh ricotta cheese

1 1/2 cups grated Gruyère cheese

2 garlic cloves, minced

1 1/2 teaspoons salt

Freshly ground black pepper

In a stockpot, combine the squash and onion and cover with cold water. Bring to a boil.

Boil for 30 minutes or until the squash and onion are tender (the squash must be tender or it will render more water in the final cooking).

Drain over a large bowl for 40 minutes. Push firmly on the vegetables to extract all the liquid. (Reserve liquid for a soup.)

Preheat the oven to 400 degrees.

In a large bowl, combine ricotta, Gruyère, garlic, salt, and pepper. Toss in the drained vegetables.

Pack the vegetables in a 3-quart baking dish.

Bake on the middle shelf of the oven for 30 minutes or until golden brown. Cool 10 minutes before serving.

Soufflé de polenta

Cornmeal Soufflé

I COOK cornmeal dishes in winter to accompany hearty stews.

SERVES 6

2 cups milk

2/3 cup medium-fine yellow
    cornmeal

4 tablespoons unsalted butter plus
    1 teaspoon for the dish

1/2 teaspoon salt

Freshly ground black pepper

3 eggs, separated

Preheat the oven to 350 degrees. Butter a 6-cup soufflé dish.

In a medium heavy-bottomed pan, bring the milk to a boil.

In a continuous stream, whisk in the cornmeal. With a large wooden spoon, stir in the butter and cook until the cornmeal is the consistency of thick cream, about 10 minutes. Season with salt and freshly ground pepper.

Remove the pan from the heat and stir in the egg yolks, one at a time.

Beat the egg whites to soft peaks and fold them in the cornmeal.

Pour the batter in the prepared soufflé dish.

Bake in the middle of the oven for 30 minutes, until puffy and golden. Serve immediately.

Soufflé de polenta aux champignons

CORNMEAL SOUFFLÉ WITH MUSHROOMS

SERVES 6

$^{1}/_{2}$ **pound portobello, or other mushrooms**

1 tablespoon olive oil

1 tablespoon minced parsley

1 large garlic clove, minced

$^{1}/_{4}$ **teaspoon salt**

Rinse the mushrooms very quickly under cold running water; pat dry and discard the tough stems (or keep them for a stock). Cut the mushrooms into ½-inch wedges.

In a large nonstick skillet, heat the oil over medium heat. Sauté the mushrooms with the parsley and garlic for 1 minute.

Sprinkle with salt, cover, and cook over low heat until tender (5 minutes).

Fold the mushrooms into the cornmeal soufflé batter and bake as above.

Galettes de polenta aux raisins

⌇

Cornmeal Galettes with Raisins

I SERVE THESE galettes as a garnish for Roasted Squabs with Shallots (page 135) and all roast fowl.

SERVES 4

$^1/_2$ cup golden raisins	$^2/_3$ cup cornmeal
$1^1/_2$ cups brewed tea	$^1/_3$ cup freshly grated Parmesan cheese
$2^1/_2$ cups milk	1 tablespoon olive oil
1 teaspoon salt	

In a small bowl, soak the raisins in the tea for 1 hour, then drain. Grease a cookie sheet and set aside.

In a saucepan, bring the milk and salt to a boil. Gradually stir in the cornmeal and cook over moderate heat for 10 minutes, stirring.

Stir in the Parmesan and raisins; cook for 1 to 2 minutes or until very thick.

Spread the polenta on the greased cookie sheet to a 12-inch square, $^1/_4$ inch thick. Set aside to cool.

Trim the edges of the polenta to make a perfect square. Cut 4 square galettes.

In a large nonstick skillet, heat the oil. Fry the galettes over medium heat until lightly browned, about 2 minutes per side.

If I make them in advance, I reheat them in the oven when dinner is ready.

SEMOLINA AND COUSCOUS are ground from durum wheat. Semolina's texture is fine; couscous is processed more coarsely. If you can't find semolina, substitute fine cornmeal.

Gnocchi à la semoule

Semolina Gnocchi

BE SURE TO buy semolina and not semolina flour. Semolina is very fine but slightly gritty; the flour is smooth.

I serve the gnocchi as a side dish with *daubes* (stews) and sometimes as a first course with morels and a morel cream sauce (see the variation, Gnocchi with Morels, below).

SERVES 8 TO 10

1 quart milk	1³/₄ cups semolina
4 tablespoons butter	3 eggs
1 teaspoon salt	1 cup grated Gruyère cheese
Freshly ground black pepper	2 teaspoons olive oil

In a large pan, combine the milk, butter, salt, and pepper. Bring to a boil. Add the semolina in a thin stream, stirring constantly with a wooden spoon.

When the mixture is very thick, remove from the heat. Whisk in the eggs, one at a time. Stir in the cheese.

On a greased surface, spread the semolina mixture into a 14-inch square, ¹/₂ inch thick. Set aside to cool.

Preheat the oven to 350 degrees.

With a large knife, trim the square and cut it into 2-inch-square gnocchi.

Dribble 1 teaspoon oil in a large baking dish and add the gnocchi and dribble another teaspoon oil over. Bake for 10 minutes or until lightly golden on top.

continued

VARIATION

Gnocchi avec morilles

GNOCCHI WITH MORELS

YOU CAN SUBSTITUTE porcini for the morels if you wish.

SERVES 8 TO 10

1¹/₂ ounces (1 cup) dried morels

1 cup heavy cream

Place the morels in a colander and scrub under cold water to remove sand. Soak them in 2 cups warm water for 1 hour

Over a bowl, strain the morel liquid through a strainer lined with paper towels and press out the water. Reserve the liquid for the cream sauce. Coarsely chop the morels and set aside.

Make the gnocchi from the above recipe, opposite. Stir the morels into the gnocchi mixture with the cheese and proceed with the above recipe.

Preheat the oven to 350 degrees.

In a large skillet, combine the morel liquid and cream. Bring to a boil and boil down to 1 cup.

Pour the sauce over the gnocchi and bake for 10 minutes. Serve immediately.

Purée de haricots blancs

White Bean Puree

ALWAYS BUY DRY *beans in a store with a big bean turnover.* The beans should be white, not yellow or brown from time spent on a shelf. Believe me, I know. I won't forget the summer of 1970 when my reputation as a cook was on the line. I planned to make cassoulet for 30 people, though I no longer remember why a cassoulet in the middle of July! The fresh beans weren't ready to be picked so I foolishly bought the bean reserve of the entire village of Valdrôme, population 73, from the only general store in the village. Too late did I realize that the beans must have been there since the last war! I cooked them and I cooked them. Half the beans remained hard.

Fortunately, I had bought many more pounds than I needed. Wayne and I spent hours picking out the uncooked beans, bean by bean! I can safely say it was the most boring chore I have ever done in the kitchen. The cassoulet was a hit, but what a price we paid!

SERVES 6

1 pound cannellini or Great Northern beans

¼ cup olive oil

6 garlic cloves, peeled

1 tablespoon minced fresh tarragon

2½ teaspoons salt

Soak the beans overnight in cold water. Drain.

Turn into a 6-quart dutch oven and cover with water. Bring to a boil. Drain.

Combine the beans, olive oil, garlic cloves, and tarragon in the dutch oven.

Pour in 5 cups of water. Cover and simmer for 1½ hours or until the beans are soft. After 30 minutes, sprinkle with the salt.

Drain the beans reserving the liquid. With ¼ cup bean liquid for each batch, process the beans in 2 batches until very smooth.

Taste and correct seasoning.

Reheat the beans in a water bath when ready to serve.

Ragoût de haricots blancs

White Bean Stew

I COULD EAT potatoes every day, and for Wayne, it's beans! I make bean stew for all seasons with fresh or dry beans, fresh or canned tomatoes. Sometimes I finish cooking this bean stew with the Roast Leg of Lamb (page 171), or I serve it with the Broiled Salmon Fillet (page 108).

SERVES 8

1$\frac{1}{2}$ pounds dry cannellini or navy beans, shelled, or 4$\frac{1}{2}$ pounds cranberry beans in their pods (about 7 cups)

$\frac{1}{3}$ cup olive oil

2 onions, thinly sliced (2 cups)

8 large garlic cloves, minced

One 28-ounce can Italian plum tomatoes, drained and chopped (reserve the liquid for a soup) or 1 pound fresh tomatoes, peeled, seeded, and chopped (see Note, page 9) (about 2 cups)

4 teaspoons salt

Soak the beans overnight in a large amount of water.

Drain the beans. In a 9-quart dutch oven, cover the beans with water and bring to a boil. Drain, and set the beans aside. (Omit soaking and parboiling the beans if fresh beans are used.)

In the dutch oven, heat the olive oil over medium heat. Add the onions and garlic. Cover and braise for 5 minutes.

Uncover, add the tomatoes, and cook for 5 minutes over medium high heat, stirring occasionally.

Add the beans and 5 cups water. Bring to a boil, lower the heat, cover, and cook for 45 to 60 minutes, until the beans are barely tender. Stir in the salt. (For the Roast Leg of Lamb, stop the cooking at this point because the beans finish cooking with the lamb.) Cover the beans and cook them over low heat for another 1$\frac{1}{2}$ hours or until very tender, adding more water if necessary. The beans should be very moist at the end of cooking.

Rizoto maison

Risotto My Way

In *La Cuisinière provençale,* J. B. Reboul, the classic authoritative Provençal cookbook author, gives recipes for rizoto (an unconventional spelling) that differ from the traditional Italian method. The liquid is poured in the rice all at once with no stirring; the method is similar to that of rice pilaf.

SERVES 6

2 cups round starchy rice, such as Arborio

4 tablespoons olive oil

2 onions, minced (2 cups)

$^1/_2$ cup tomato sauce (page 8 or page 10)

4 cups Light Broth (page 11)

$1^1/_2$ teaspoons salt

Freshly ground black pepper

Pinch of ground nutmeg

A bouquet garni (1 sprig each of parsley and thyme and 1 bay leaf tied with 1 halved celery stalk)

$^1/_2$ cup grated Parmesan cheese

Rinse the rice under cold running water. Drain.

In a large nonstick skillet, heat the olive oil over medium high heat. Sauté the onion and rice for 1 minute.

Stir in the tomato sauce. Add the broth, salt, pepper, nutmeg, and bouquet garni.

Cover tightly and cook very slowly for 20 minutes or until the rice is tender.

Discard the bouquet garni.

Reheat with the cheese. Taste and correct seasoning.

Serve immediately.

Desserts

Early June

Tarte au clafoutis de cerises   •   261
    (Cherry Clafoutis in a Tart)

Tarte campagnarde aux cerises   •   262
    (Country Cherry Tart)

Late June and Early July

Tarte aux abricots   •   263
    (Apricot Tart)

July

Tarte aux clafoutis de framboises   •   264
    (Raspberry Clafoutis in a Tart)

August

Tarte aux myrtilles   •   265
    (Blueberry Tart)

Late August and September

Tarte aux figues fraîches   •   266
    (Fresh Fig Tart)

September

Tarte renversée aux prunes   •   267
    (Caramelized Upside-Down Plum Tart)

October

Galette aux pommes   •   268
    (Apple Galette)

November

Tarte aux poires et aux amandes   •   269
    (Pear and Almond Tart)

ALL KINDS OF FRUIT trees grow in the Midi; a bowl of fruit often serves for dessert. There is a great variety: from cherries, berries, melons, apples, pears, and peaches (plus a few grapes that escape the wineries) to such exotic fruits as oranges, clementines, lemons, kiwi, and persimmons.

In winter, dessert is often the famous Provençal candied fruits. Candied Cavaillon melons, peaches, apricots, clementines, lemons, all grace the windows of pastry shops and the market stalls. They are beautiful to behold and they taste good too.

On Tarts

I TAKE ADVANTAGE of seasonal fruits to bake tarts year round using a standard pâte brisée, the French version of short crust.

Tarts are easy to prepare once the dough is made and rolled out. I keep several unbaked shells in my freezer. The pastry freezes well, and there is no need to defrost it before baking. But once the finished tart is baked do not refrigerate, which toughens the crust, and do not cover the tart with plastic wrap, which makes the crust soggy. Just invert a plate over the tart and set it aside on the kitchen counter.

I usually bake my tarts in a pan with a removable bottom, to make serving easier. While the tart is still hot, I place it on a tall jar with a wide lid, such as a large can of tomatoes. Run a knife blade along the edge of the tart to unstick if necessary. Juicy fruits such as rhubarb, cherries, or apricots will stick.

Neophyte pie bakers often worry that they'll miss creating a perfect circle and think themselves incapable of doing pastries. I am very relaxed about it; if it tears, I patch it. After all, in France it is called just that: broken dough (*pâte brisée*). I don't worry and I don't let my husband intimidate me the way he did his poor aunt Eulah, the baker in the Marshall family.

Years ago Wayne was watching Aunt Eulah roll out pastry, his eyes level with the top of the table. Aunt Eulah, very frazzled that day, was making a mess. Wayne asked: "You really don't know what you're doing, do you, Aunt Eulah?" Wayne is still alive to tell the story, but it was a close call.

Pâte brisée

Short Crust Dough

IF YOU ARE a novice, wait for cool weather to learn how to make pastry dough; it will be easier to handle the dough. Keep flour in the freezer during the summer months.

MAKES 10 OUNCES OF DOUGH, ENOUGH FOR ONE 10-INCH
TART SHELL PLUS TRIMMINGS

8 tablespoons (1 stick) unsalted butter

1 cup unbleached all-purpose flour

Pinch of salt

2 to 3 tablespoons cold water, depending on the weather

Cut the butter into small pieces and place in the freezer for 5 minutes.

In the bowl of a food processor, combine the flour, salt, and butter. Process for 10 seconds, add 2 tablespoons water in humid weather or 3 tablespoons in dry weather.

Process for another 10 seconds or until the mixture looks like cornmeal.

Dump the mixture on a table or counter and bind a small amount at a time with the heel of your hand, using a sliding motion to incorporate the butter and flour smoothly.

Gather the dough into a ball and flatten it. Wrap in wax paper and refrigerate for 15 minutes, just long enough to firm up the butter.

Flour a work surface and rolling pin. Roll the dough to a 13-inch circle, always making sure there is flour under the dough and on the rolling pin, otherwise the dough will stick to the pastry surface or to the rolling pin.

Line a 10-inch tart pan with the dough. Trim the excess (keep it frozen until you have enough scraps to make another tart shell). Prick the bottom and refrigerate the unbaked tart shell for 2 hours or freeze it until ready to bake.

THIS IS ONE basic tart shell recipe, cooked in 2 ways. The Partially Prebaked Tart Shell is used when the tart will be filled and then baked again. The Fully Prebaked Tart Shell is used when the contents of the tart are fresh (as in the case of a fresh fruit tart) and will not be baked after filling. I specify which type of shell to use in the recipes that follow.

A Partially Prebaked Tart Shell

Preheat the oven to 400 degrees.

Line the tart shell with aluminum foil and fill it with dry beans.

Place the tart shell in the middle of the oven and bake for 15 minutes. Remove the beans and foil. Bake 5 to 10 minutes to dry out the bottom without coloring.

A Fully Prebaked Tart Shell

Bake 10 to 15 minutes after removing the beans and foil, above. For a fully prebaked tart shell, the bottom of the shell should be uniformly light golden.

Tarte aux clémentines

Clementine Tart

ALL ALONG THE hilly back country of Golfe-Juan on the Riviera, residents with small gardens tack signs on their doors: CLÉMENTINES À VENDRE. January is the month of clementines, and there is such an abundance that people have to find one way or another to unload clementines. Pastry shops sell marvelous candied clementines. A real treat awaits you if you are in Provence in wintertime: candied clementines. Bite into the fruit, rind included, and sweet nectar will drip from your lips.

If you can't find clementines, substitute seedless mandarins or tangerines.

SERVES 6

2 cups sugar

6 to 8 clementines, sliced
⅛ inch thick or enough slices
to cover a 10-inch tart

4 teaspoons cornstarch, sifted

1 egg yolk

1 cup freshly squeezed orange juice

2 tablespoons butter

One 10-inch Partially Prebaked
Tart Shell (page 253)

½ cup heated apricot jam

Preheat the oven to 400 degrees.

In a large saucepan, bring 2 cups water and 2 cups sugar to a boil. Boil 3 minutes to dissolve the sugar. Add the clementine slices and simmer for 30 minutes or until the slices are soft. Set aside to cool in the pan.

Sift the cornstarch into a mixing bowl. Place the egg yolk in a second mixing bowl.

In a medium pan, bring the orange juice to a boil. Briskly whisk half the orange juice into the cornstarch and add the egg yolk.

Bring the remaining orange juice back to a boil and quickly whisk in the cornstarch mixture until very thick, about 1 minute.

Off the heat, whisk in the butter. Set aside to cool.

Pour the custard on the partially prebaked tart shell. Drain the clementine slices and arrange them on top of the tart.

Bake in the middle of the oven for 30 to 35 minutes, until the custard is set.

Brush apricot jam over the sides of the tart and on top of the poached clementines.

Tarte princesse à la confiture d'abricots

Almond and Apricot Jam Tart

IN LATE WINTER, between the end of apple and pear season but before the red fruits of the spring, I make apricot jam tarts with almonds.

SERVES 6

1 cup unskinned almonds

8 tablespoons (1 stick) unsalted butter, at room temperature

$1/2$ cup sugar

3 eggs, separated

$1/8$ teaspoon pure almond extract

$3/4$ cup apricot jam or preserves, heated

One 10-inch Partially Prebaked Tart Shell (page 253)

Preheat the oven to 425 degrees.

In a food processor, pulse the almonds until coarsely ground.

Add the butter, sugar, egg yolks, and almond extract. Process until smooth.

Beat the egg whites until firm but not dry. Fold a third of the beaten whites into the almond mixture.

Fold the almond mixture into the remaining beaten egg whites.

Spread the apricot jam on the bottom of the partially prebaked tart shell. Pour the almond mixture over it, spreading it evenly on top of the apricot jam.

Bake for 20 minutes until golden brown. Cover loosely with foil to prevent overbrowning and bake for 10 to 15 minutes more or until the filling is set in the center.

Tarte aux citrons confits

Candied Lemon Tart

SERVES 6

3 eggs

3/4 cup sugar

4 tablespoons unsalted butter, at
 room temperature

2 tablespoons grated lemon peel

2/3 cup freshly squeezed lemon juice

One 10-inch Partially Prebaked
 Tart Shell (page 253)

8 candied lemon slices (see below)

Confectioners' sugar

In a bowl of a heavy-duty mixer, beat the eggs and sugar at medium speed until thick and foamy, about 5 minutes.

Gradually beat in the butter, the grated lemon peel, and the lemon juice.

Pour the mixture into a large saucepan. Cook over medium heat until the mixture thickens, whisking occasionally, about 5 minutes.

Transfer to a bowl and refrigerate until cold, about 1 hour.

Preheat the oven to 400 degrees.

Spread the cold custard in the partially prebaked tart shell.

Bake for 30 to 40 minutes in the middle of the oven.

Arrange the candied lemon slices over the tart.

Just before serving, sprinkle with confectioners' sugar.

continued

Citrons confits

CANDIED LEMONS

THESE CANDIED LEMONS also make an attractive simple dessert, served with a bowl of sour cream and fresh raspberries.

SERVES 6

1 cup sugar

2 lemons, cut into ⅛-inch-thick slices

In a large stainless steel pan, combine 1 cup sugar and 1 cup water. Bring to a boil to dissolve the sugar. Add the lemon slices. Cover and cook over medium heat for 30 minutes. Remove from the heat and let the lemon slices cool in the syrup.

To serve as a dessert, transfer the cooled candied lemon slices to a serving bowl.

Tarte aux fraises

Strawberry Tart

MY FAVORITE STRAWBERRY tart is made without custard. I fill the baked tart shell with strawberries at the last minute, just before serving, otherwise the strawberries (especially during hot humid days) will weep and juice will seep through the crust, making it soggy.

SERVES 6

¹/₂ cup strawberry jam, heated

One 10-inch Fully prebaked Tart Shell (page 253)

2 pints strawberries, hulled

A bowl of sour cream

Brush strawberry jam in the tart shell.

If the strawberries are large, shape them into smaller strawberries and eat the trimmings or make the compote on page 283.

Dip each strawberry in the warm jam and fill the tart shell. Pass a bowl of sour cream along with the tart.

Tarte à la rhubarbe

Rhubarb Tart

THIS TART IS not so pretty when it comes out of the oven. But as soon as you bite into it, you will forget its look.

SERVES 6

6 tablespoons coarsely
chopped almonds

$^2/_3$ cup sugar

One 10-inch Partially Prebaked
Tart Shell (page 253)

$1^1/_2$ pounds rhubarb, cut up in
$^1/_4$-inch cubes (4 cups)

2 teaspoons unsalted butter, cut
into shavings

Confectioners' sugar

Preheat the oven to 425 degrees.

Combine the chopped almonds with 3 tablespoons sugar and spread on the partially prebaked tart shell.

Pile the rhubarb on top of the almond and sugar mixture. Sprinkle the remaining sugar on the rhubarb and scatter shavings of butter on top.

Bake the tart on top of a cookie sheet on the middle rack of the oven for 30 minutes. The edge of the tart will be slightly colored and the fruit will have shrunk.

Before serving, sprinkle with confectioners' sugar.

Tarte au clafoutis de cerises

∽

Cherry Clafoutis in a Tart

IF YOU DON'T OWN a cherry pitter, put the cherries in a jelly roll pan and crush them slightly with the bottom of a bowl; the pits will pop out easily.

SERVES 6

1 pound black or Bing cherries, pitted

One 10-inch Partially Prebaked Tart Shell (page 253)

1/2 cup sugar

2 eggs

2 tablespoons flour

1/2 cup sour cream

Preheat the oven to 400 degrees.

Spread the pitted cherries evenly on the bottom of a partially prebaked tart shell.

In a mixing bowl, combine the sugar, eggs, flour, and sour cream and mix thoroughly. Pour over the cherries.

Place the tart mold on a cookie sheet and bake for 30 minutes or until golden.

Eat warm.

Tarte campagnarde aux cerises

Country Cherry Tart

DR. EDOUARD DE POMIANE, a master storyteller who delighted thousands of radio listeners in the 1930s, warned his listeners on one of his shows that "when you open the oven door you will have a shock. It is not a pretty sight. The edges of the tart are slightly burned and the top layer of cherries blackened in places . . . it will be received without much enthusiasm for, frankly, it is not too prepossessing. . . . Don't be discouraged. Cut the first slice and the juice will run out. Now try it. A surprise. The pastry is neither crisp nor soggy, and just tinged with cherry juice. The cherries have kept all their flavor and the juice is not sticky—just pure cherry juice."

In Nyons during cooking classes, we'd eat part of the tart warm for tea, and the rest cold (but never refrigerated) the next morning for breakfast.

SERVES 6

1 cup Potato Bread Dough, refrigerated after the first rise (page 76) or 1 cup St. Tropez Cake batter after the first rise (page 271)

2 cups pitted black or Bing cherries

$^1/_2$ cup sugar

1 tablespoon (or more) butter, cut into small pieces

Preheat the oven to 425 degrees.

Spread the dough with your hands in a 9 by 6-inch baking pan. Cover the pan with a plastic bag and set aside to rise for about 1 hour.

Pit the cherries right on the dough.

Sprinkle the sugar over the cherries and scatter the butter on top.

Bake for approximately 25 minutes, until the tart is puffy and golden.

Eat warm or cold.

Tarte aux abricots

Apricot Tart

WHEN YOU TRAVEL through the Baronnies region in northeast Provence, you will see drawings of apricots on billboards, proclaiming them the "Orange of Provence." We are very proud of our apricots and for the very good reason that they are delicious. I have an apricot tree that provides for several quarts of apricot jam as well as an apricot tart every day of the apricot season. One day last summer, door and window open, I left the kitchen for a while with an apricot tart freshly made on the table. I came back to an empty tart plate and a cat in the garden smugly laughing at me as he was licking his paws and chops.

SERVES 6

½ cup sugar

2 pounds ripe apricots, halved and pitted

One 10-inch Partially Prebaked Tart Shell (page 253)

2 medium eggs

2 tablespoons flour

½ cup sour cream or crème fraîche

Preheat the oven to 400 degrees.

Sprinkle ¼ cup sugar over the apricot halves, cut side up. Set aside for 30 minutes.

Arrange the apricot halves, cut side up, slightly overlapping in the partially prebaked tart shell.

In a mixing bowl, combine the remaining sugar, eggs, flour, and cream and mix thoroughly. Pour over the apricots.

Place the tart mold on a cookie sheet and bake for 30 minutes or until golden.

Eat warm.

Tarte aux clafoutis de framboises

Raspberry Clafoutis in a Tart

SERVES 6

10 tablespoons sugar

3 cups raspberries

2 eggs

4 tablespoons flour

1/4 cup heavy cream

1/4 cup milk

1 tablespoon framboise liqueur

One 10-inch Partially Prebaked
Tart Shell (page 253)

1 tablespoon confectioners' sugar

1 cup sour cream mixed with
1 tablespoon sugar

Preheat the oven to 425 degrees.

Sprinkle 2 tablespoons sugar on the raspberries and let stand for 30 minutes.

In a bowl, whisk the eggs and flour until blended. Whisk in 8 tablespoons sugar, cream, milk, and the framboise liqueur.

Fold the raspberries into the mixture and pour into the partially prebaked tart shell. Place the tart mold on a cookie sheet lined with aluminum foil.

Bake the tart for 15 minutes; the raspberries will be very dark. Set aside to cool.

When ready to serve, set the broiler on high.

Sprinkle the tart with 1 tablespoon confectioners' sugar and place under the broiler for 1 minute to caramelize the top.

Serve with the sweetened sour cream.

Tarte aux myrtilles

Blueberry Tart

SERVES 6

1/4 cup whole unskinned
almonds

6 tablespoons granulated sugar

2 tablespoons all-purpose flour

One 10-inch unbaked tart shell
(page 253)

4 cups blueberries

1 tablespoon confectioners' sugar

1 cup sour cream mixed with
2 tablespoons sugar

Preheat the oven to 450 degrees.

In the bowl of a food processor, process the almonds, 3 tablespoons sugar, and the flour until the almonds are finely ground.

Sprinkle the almond mixture in the unbaked tart shell and cover with the blueberries. Sprinkle the remaining 3 tablespoons sugar over the berries.

Place the tart on the bottom rack of the oven and lower the temperature to 400 degrees. Bake for about 30 minutes or until the bottom crust is golden (peek by gently lifting the tart with a long narrow spatula or the blade of a long knife).

Sprinkle the tart with confectioners' sugar before serving it with a bowl of sweetened sour cream.

Tarte aux figues fraîches

Fresh Fig Tart

SERVES 6

$^1/_3$ cup unpeeled almonds

$^1/_3$ cup sugar

1 small egg

3 tablespoons unsalted butter

2 teaspoons dark rum

One 10-inch Partially Prebaked Tart Shell (page 253)

$1^1/_2$ pounds unpeeled figs, cut into 8 wedges

Preheat the oven to 425 degrees.

In the bowl of a food processor, process the almonds until finely ground.

Add the sugar, egg, butter, and rum. Process for 1 minute. Refrigerate until firm, about 15 minutes.

Spread the almond butter on the bottom of the partially prebaked tart shell.

Arrange each fig, cut side up, on top of the almond butter.

Place a cookie sheet under the tart mold and bake for 30 minutes. Serve at room temperature.

Tarte renversée aux prunes

Caramelized Upside-Down Plum Tart

THIS TART WORKS best with small dark purple plums.

I make this tart in a 9-inch cast-iron skillet or a nonstick pan with a metal handle.

SERVES 6

4 tablespoons unsalted butter

½ cup sugar

1½ pounds dark purple plums,
    halved and pitted

Short Crust Dough (*Pâte brisée*)
    (page 252)

1 teaspoon heavy cream

1 teaspoon sugar

1 cup sour cream mixed with
    2 tablespoons sugar

In a 9-inch cast-iron or nonstick skillet, combine butter, sugar, and plums. Over medium high heat, caramelize the plums until the juices have thickened, about 20 minutes. Set aside until cool.

Preheat the oven to 425 degrees.

Roll out the Short Crust dough to a 12-inch circle. Drape the dough over a rolling pin and flip it on the cooled plums. Brush off excess flour.

With your fingertips, make a rim on top of the plums with the dough hanging over the pan.

Prick the dough with the tines of a fork and brush cream and sugar over it.

Bake the tart for 20 to 25 minutes or until the top is golden brown.

Unmold immediately on a serving dish. Eat warm or cold.

Serve with the sweetened sour cream.

Galette aux pommes

Apple Galette

A GALETTE IS a free-form tart. I made this galette once on the spur of the moment, after dinner. I had cold pastry dough in the refrigerator and apples in a bowl. We ate the galette hot from the oven and it was a real treat. For a dinner party I roll the dough in the afternoon, assemble it before dinner, and bake it during dinner.

SERVES 6

Short Crust Dough (*Pâte brisée*) (page 252)

$^{1}/_{2}$ cup apricot jam or preserves

2 unpeeled Gala or Golden Delicious apples (about 1 pound), cut into $^{1}/_{8}$- to $^{1}/_{16}$-inch-thick slices

1 tablespoon sugar

2 teaspoons unsalted butter, cut into shavings

1 cup sour cream mixed with 1 tablespoon sugar

Preheat the oven to 450 degrees.

Roll the dough into a rough 14-inch circle and trim it to a 13-inch circle. Refrigerate on a cookie sheet until ready to use.

In a small pan, heat the apricot jam with 2 teaspoons water.

Brush half of the warm jam over the pastry dough.

Arrange slightly overlapping apple slices on the dough, leaving a 1-inch border. Fold the free edge over the apples.

Brush the remaining jam over the apples and the pastry edge. Sprinkle the apples with sugar.

Scatter shavings of butter on top of the apples.

Place the tart on the bottom rack of the oven and lower the temperature to 400 degrees. Bake for about 30 minutes, or until the bottom crust is golden (peek by gently lifting the tart with a long narrow spatula or with the blade of a long knife).

Serve with a bowl of sweetened sour cream.

Tarte aux poires et aux amandes

Pear and Almond Tart

I BUY PEARS a little underripe and decorate my kitchen table with them. When they are ripe, I bake them.

SERVES 6

½ cup whole unskinned almonds

4 tablespoons sugar

One 10-inch Partially Prebaked Tart Shell (page 253)

4 juicy pears, peeled, cored, and cut into 8 wedges each (see Note)

¾ cup warm orange marmalade

1 cup sour cream mixed with 2 tablespoons sugar

Preheat the oven to 450 degrees.

In the bowl of a food processor, process the almonds and sugar until the almonds are coarsely chopped.

Sprinkle half the almond mixture into the partially prebaked tart shell.

Arrange the pears cut side up, wedges overlapping in the tart shell.

Brush ½ cup warm orange marmalade over the pears. Sprinkle the remaining almond mixture on top of the pears.

Place the tart on the bottom rack of the oven and lower the temperature to 400 degrees. Bake for about 30 minutes or until the bottom crust is golden (peek by gently lifting the tart with a long narrow spatula or with the blade of a long knife).

Transfer the tart to a rack and brush the sides with remaining marmalade.

Serve with a bowl of sweetened sour cream.

NOTE:

If the pears are not totally ripe and you can't wait, combine ½ cup sugar and 1 cup water in a large skillet. Boil for 3 minutes. Add the pears and poach for 5 minutes. Drain and proceed with the recipe.

Tarte aux noix

Nut Tart

IN NYONS, I make the tart with walnuts; in New York, I use pecans. The nuts are interchangeable in this tart, so you choose.

SERVES 6

1 cup heavy cream

⅓ cup sugar

2 cups not too finely ground
    pecans or walnuts

One 10-inch Partially Prebaked
    Tart Shell (page 253)

Preheat the oven to 400 degrees.

Beat the heavy cream until firm. Fold in the sugar and nuts.

Fill the partially prebaked tart shell with the nut-cream mixture.

Bake the tart on top of a cookie sheet for 25 to 30 minutes or until golden brown. The filling will look moist; it sets as it cools.

Tarte St. Tropez

St. Tropez Cake

ST. TROPEZ IS known not only for the beautiful people but for this beautiful cake.

A flat cake made with a yeast dough, the St. Tropez is filled with whipped cream. Nan Chisholm, who was helping test and retest this dessert, thought she would never bother making it. It sounded too plain to be appealing! "I was wrong," Nan admitted, "I was so impressed by the taste and simplicity of the cake that I made it the very next week (in a heart-shaped pan for Valentine's Day) and all my friends loved it as well." The cake can be made a day in advance.

You need a 4-cup cake mold; I use a 10-inch layer cake pan to make a large flat cake.

SERVES 8

2 teaspoons active dry yeast

$^{1}/_{4}$ cup lukewarm milk

1 teaspoon sugar plus
  2 tablespoons

2 large eggs

7 tablespoons unsalted butter,
  softened

$1^{3}/_{4}$ cups unbleached all-purpose
  flour

$^{1}/_{2}$ teaspoon salt

FOR THE GLAZE

1 teaspoon milk mixed with
  1 tablespoon sugar

FOR THE SYRUP

$^{3}/_{4}$ cup sugar

$^{3}/_{4}$ cup water

2 tablespoons rum

FOR THE FILLING

1 cup heavy cream, whipped

FOR THE TOPPING

Confectioners' sugar

continued

In winter, I rinse my mixing bowl under hot water and dry it before making a yeast dough.

In a large mixing bowl, combine the yeast with the milk, adding 1 teaspoon sugar. Set aside for 10 minutes.

Add 2 eggs and the soft butter to the yeast.

In a small mixing bowl, combine 2 tablespoons sugar, flour, and salt.

With a wooden spoon, gradually beat 1 to 2 tablespoons flour at a time into the yeast-egg-butter mixture. At first the batter will look curdled, but as you add flour, it will smooth out. Beat the batter until smooth; it should have the moist consistency of cream puff dough. Stop adding flour if the dough changes consistency. (This can be done in a heavy-duty mixer but not in the food processor, which will make the texture of the cake too dense.)

Cover the bowl with plastic wrap and set aside to rise in a warm place until it doubles in size, about 1 hour.

Grease and sugar a layer cake pan 10 inches wide and 2 inches deep or any 4-cup mold.

Spread the batter in the pan with your fingers. Brush the milk and sugar glaze over the top of the tart.

Cover the pan loosely with a large plastic bag, making sure that the dough does not touch the bag. Set aside in a warm place to fill the pan, about 30 minutes.

Preheat the oven to 375 degrees.

Bake the tart for 25 minutes or until golden brown.

Meanwhile, prepare the syrup: combine sugar and water in a saucepan. Bring to a boil. Boil 2 to 3 minutes. Turn off the heat and add the rum.

Transfer the cake to a baking rack. Set aside to cool for 10 minutes.

With a long bread knife, split the cake in half sandwich-like or into 3 layers if the cake was baked in a deeper pan.

With a fork, prick all over the inside of the cake halves and sprinkle the rum syrup.

It can be done 1 day in advance up to this point. Put the cake halves together and wrap in plastic but do not refrigerate. Set aside on a kitchen counter.

Beat the heavy cream and refrigerate in a strainer over a mixing bowl (as it stands in the refrigerator, whipped cream weeps).

Just before serving dessert, spread the bottom half of the cake with the whipped cream. Cover with the top half of the cake and sprinkle lots of confectioners' sugar on top.

If you have leftovers, do not refrigerate the cake; wrap it in plastic. If refrigerated, the cake loses its light texture.

Charlotte aux myrtilles et aux framboises

Blueberry and Raspberry Summer Pudding

DURING MY SUMMERS in Nyons, I entertain many visitors. It's a good time to try new recipes, but I seem to rely on my favorite summer charlotte, inspired by the English fruit pudding.

SERVES 8

$6^{1}/_{2}$ cups blueberries

$^{3}/_{4}$ cup sugar

$6^{1}/_{2}$ cups raspberries

$6^{1}/_{4}$-inch-thick packaged white bread slices, cut into thirds

FOR THE GARNISH

$^{1}/_{4}$ cup blueberries

$^{1}/_{4}$ cup raspberries

1 cup sour cream, sweetened with 2 tablespoons sugar

In a large nonstick skillet, combine the blueberries, sugar, and $1^{1}/_{2}$ cups water. Stir and bring to a boil. Boil until the berries begin to swell, about 1 to 2 minutes.

With a slotted spoon, transfer the berries to a strainer set over a bowl.

Add the raspberries to the simmering liquid and poach for 1 minute.

Transfer the raspberries to the strainer.

With the back of the slotted spoon, press gently on the fruits to extract some of their juice.

Add the berry juice collected in the bowl to the liquid in the skillet. Bring to a boil and reduce to $1^{1}/_{4}$ cups, until a syrup consistency is achieved, about 15 minutes. Set aside to cool.

Oil a 6-cup soufflé mold or charlotte mold. Line the sides of the pan with bread strips.

Pack half the berries into the prepared mold and pour $^{1}/_{2}$ cup syrup over them. Add the remaining berries and pour $^{1}/_{2}$ cup syrup over them.

Tap the pan against the counter. Trim the bread flush with the fruits and cover the top with more bread.

Pour the remaining ¼ cup syrup over the bread. Cover with a plate. Place a weight on the plate and refrigerate overnight.

Unmold onto a serving platter. Garnish with whole berries and serve with the sweetened sour cream.

Rochers à la noix de coco

Coconut Macaroons

A CERTAIN AMOUNT of confusion exists because French macaroons are what we call meringues (page 277). Don't worry about the names, these cookies are all delicious.

Make 1 batch of cookies at a time. Do not attempt to double the recipe, it just doesn't work; the batter gets too loose. Buy unsweetened grated coconut in health food stores.

MAKES 20 COOKIES

$1^2/_3$ cups unsweetened grated coconut

$^1/_3$ cup sugar

2 large eggs

1 tablespoon melted butter

Preheat the oven to 350 degrees.

In a mixing bowl, combine the grated coconut and sugar. Blend with a fork.

Beat the eggs and measure a little less than ½ cup (discard the surplus).

Combine the eggs and butter in the coconut mixture until blended.

Grease 1 cookie sheet. Make 20 mounds, spacing them every 1 inch on the cookie sheet.

Bake on the middle shelf of the oven for 20 minutes or until lightly golden brown on top.

Gently, pry them loose and set aside to cool on a baking rack.

FROZEN EGG WHITES are perfect for making almond meringue cookies. My friend Barbara Fenzl taught me how to freeze individual egg whites in a 12-cup muffin tin. When the egg whites are frozen, she turns the muffin tin upside down under hot water for just a second to dislodge them. Then she stores them in a freezer bag. Whenever she needs egg whites, she just takes out the number she needs and sets them aside to thaw.

Macarons fourrés au chocolat

Almond Meringue Cookies with a Chocolate Filling

IN FRANCE, MACAROONS are not made with coconut but with an almond meringue. When baked for a short time at high temperature the meringue cookie stays chewy. Two macaroons are stuck together to make a cookie sandwich with chocolate filling. They freeze very well. Do not try to double or triple the recipe unless you have a professional mixer. Ask my friend Milan Segall, who tried making 100 meringues in one shot in his home mixer and created a royal mess. He finally followed the recipe exactly and was very successful.

MAKES 18 TO 20 CHOCOLATE-FILLED MERINGUE COOKIES

½ cup heavy cream	1 cup unpeeled almonds
4 ounces bittersweet chocolate, broken into small pieces	½ cup egg whites (4 to 5 egg whites)
1 tablespoon coarsely chopped unpeeled toasted hazelnuts	3 tablespoons granulated sugar
	2 cups sifted confectioners' sugar

For the chocolate filling, in a medium pan, bring the cream to a boil. Add the chocolate and stir until melted over medium heat.

Fold in the hazelnuts. Refrigerate until stiff enough to spread, about 30 minutes.

Preheat the oven to 425 degrees (350 degrees for a convection oven).

Line 2 cookie sheets with parchment or wax paper.

continued

In the food processor, process the almonds until very fine (yields 1 cup).

In the bowl of a heavy-duty mixer, beat the egg whites until soft peaks form. Add the granulated sugar and beat until stiff and shiny.

With a rubber spatula, fold the confectioners' sugar and 1 cup almond powder into the whites. The mixture will become slightly runny.

Fit a pastry bag with $1/4$ -inch tip and pipe out 1-inch rounds 1 inch apart on the lined cookie sheets.

Put an empty cookie sheet on the top rack of the oven to prevent the tops of the meringues from burning.

Bake the meringues in the middle of the oven for 15 minutes, or until they are light golden in color.

Working quickly with a pastry scraper, remove the macaroons to a baking rack.

To assemble the macaroons, spread chocolate filling on the bottom of the meringues and make a small sandwich with two meringues of the same size.

Refrigerate until ready to serve or freeze them and remove from the freezer 1 hour before eating.

Soupe aux fraises

Strawberry Compote

WHEN STRAWBERRIES OR other berries are not perfect, I make a compote with them.

SERVES 8

2 pints strawberries

¼ cup sugar plus 1 tablespoon

¼ cup currant jelly or
    strawberry or raspberry jam

¼ cup crème de cassis

1 tablespoon lemon juice

1 cup sour cream

1 teaspoon framboise liqueur or
    kirsch

Mint sprigs

In a strainer, toss the strawberries under cold water. Pat dry with paper towels. Hull and quarter the strawberries.

In a large bowl, combine the strawberries, ¼ cup sugar, and the currant jelly or jam. Pour the crème de cassis and the lemon juice over the strawberries. Cover and refrigerate for up to 4 hours.

Combine the sour cream with 1 tablespoon sugar and the liqueur or kirsch.

Spoon the berries into parfait glasses. Decorate the top with a spoonful of sweetened sour cream; decorate with a sprig of mint.

Pruneaux au vin

❧

Prunes Poached in Wine

JEAN LUC ABRAS, our friend and Wayne's first flute teacher, is my second in command during September cooking classes at the château. He spends considerable time checking wineries in the region and buys samples for our numerous tastings of local Côtes du Rhône. With leftover samples, he makes this very simple dessert of poached prunes. In the States, I buy large prunes in bulk.

SERVES 6

2 cups red Côtes du Rhône
wine or California zinfandel

$^1/_2$ cup sugar

$^3/_4$ pound California prunes

1 orange, cut into $^1/_2$-inch-
thick slices

One $^1/_8$-inch-thick slice lemon

1 cinnamon stick

1 cup sour cream mixed with
2 tablespoons sugar

In a mixing bowl, combine wine and sugar. Add the prunes, orange, and lemon. Cover and set aside overnight.

Pour the fruits and wine into a large saucepan. Add the cinnamon and bring to a boil.

Over medium high heat, cook the fruits for 20 minutes, turning the prunes over to cook evenly.

Drain the fruits in a kitchen sieve over a bowl; transfer the prunes to a serving bowl. Discard the cinnamon stick and press the orange and lemon over the wine to extract all the juice.

Reduce the wine over high heat for 2 to 3 minutes or until slightly syrupy (yields $^3/_4$ cup).

Pour the wine over the prunes and refrigerate overnight.

Serve with a bowl of sour cream and sugar with a plate of Coconut Macaroons (page 276).

Confiture d'abricots

Apricot Jam

AT THE CHÂTEAU in late June and early July, I make quarts and quarts of apricot jam in a dutch oven. Sometimes I do not even bother to transfer the jam to jars; I pour it into varying sizes of tians (Provençal crockery bowls) and keep it refrigerated. It disappears very fast for breakfast with croissants, for dessert on ice cream, or on top of whipped fresh cheese.

Comes mid-July, everybody is busy making jam. Supermarket shelves where the "jam" sugar is stocked are emptied. The French use a special sugar mixed with citric acid and pectin for jam. For $2\frac{1}{4}$ pounds of granulated sugar, $\frac{1}{4}$ ounce each of pectin and citric acid (found in pharmacies or supermarkets) are added to the sugar. If you don't want to bother with it, cook the jam longer, to 235 degrees on a candy thermometer.

I like chunky pieces of apricots in jam but cut the apricots smaller if you wish.

MAKES 8 CUPS

4 pounds halved and pitted ripe apricots (12 cups)

3 pounds sugar

$\frac{1}{3}$ cup lemon juice

In a 9-quart dutch oven, combine the apricots, sugar, and lemon juice. Stir with a wooden spoon to coat the fruit.

Cook uncovered over low heat, slowly dissolving the sugar. Stir occasionally.

When the sugar is dissolved, turn up the heat and cook to 210 degrees on a candy thermometer, about $\frac{1}{2}$ hour, for sugar with pectin and 235 degrees for sugar without pectin.

How to Seal Fruit Jam with Paraffin

Boil water in a tea kettle and pour it over the empty jars. Drain.

Fill the jars with the jam, leaving $1/2$ inch free at the top.

In a 1-quart aluminum container, melt $1/2$ pound paraffin set in a water bath (a skillet bigger than the foil container with water in it).

Pour $1/4$-inch-thick layer of melted paraffin over the preserves and wrap the top of the jars with a pretty Provençal print before stacking them in a larder.

Délice d'été

~

Summer Delight

THIS SIMPLE DESSERT is refreshing on hot summer days.

SERVES 4

½ cup fresh goat cheese or fresh ricotta cheese

¼ cup drained plain yogurt

2 tablespoons sugar or more

½ cup blackberry, black currant, or red currant coulis (pages 285, 286, or 287)

1 cup raspberries, blackberries, or blueberries

In a food processor, process the cheese and yogurt until smooth. Add sugar to taste.

Pour coulis on individual dessert plates, tilting them to spread the coulis evenly.

Mound cheese in the center of the plate.

Sprinkle berries over the cheese and serve with Coconut Macaroons (page 276) or Almond Meringue Cookies with a Chocolate Filling (page 277).

Sirop pour coulis

Sugar Syrup for Fruit Sauce

SUGAR SYRUP KEEPS for several weeks in the refrigerator. It's helpful to have it on hand during the summer when sorbets and fruit coulis are in demand.

MAKES 1 CUP

1 cup water

1 cup sugar

In a saucepan, combine water and sugar. Bring to a boil. Do not stir. Keep it at a gentle boil for 4 minutes.

Set aside to cool completely. Bottle it, cap it, and refrigerate.

Coulis de mûres

Blackberry Sauce

THE BLACKBERRY COULIS will keep refrigerated up to 2 weeks.

MAKES 1 CUP SAUCE

1 cup blackberries

**¼ to ⅓ cup Sugar Syrup
for Fruit Sauce (opposite)**

In a food processor, process the blackberries for 1 minute. (If the blackberries have lots of seeds, especially wild blackberries, press the coulis through a kitchen sieve to discard the seeds.)

Gradually add sugar syrup to the blackberry puree until it is sweet enough to your taste.

Refrigerate.

Coulis de cassis

Black Currant Sauce

MAKES 1 CUP SAUCE

1$\frac{1}{4}$ cups fresh cassis berries

$\frac{1}{4}$ cup Sugar Syrup for Fruit
Sauce (page 284)

Process the cassis berries in a food processor for 2 minutes.

Strain through a kitchen sieve, discarding skins and seeds (yields $\frac{3}{4}$ cup cassis puree).

Whisk $\frac{1}{4}$ cup syrup in the cassis puree.

Refrigerate until ready to serve.

Coulis de groseilles

Red Currant Sauce

MAKES $^1/_2$ CUP SAUCE

8 ounces fresh red currants
   (1$^1/_4$ cups)

$^1/_4$ to $^1/_2$ cup Sugar Syrup for
   Fruit Sauce (page 284)

1 teaspoon freshly squeezed
   lemon juice

Process the currants in a food processor for 2 minutes.

Press through a kitchen sieve, discarding skins and seeds (yields about $^1/_2$ cup red currant puree).

Whisk the syrup into the currant puree with the lemon juice.

Refrigerate until ready to serve.

INDEX

squid and bean salad, 56–57
stews:
of baby artichokes with white onions and garlic, 195
beef, from the Camargue, 152–153
of monkfish and wild mushrooms, 107
Provençal tuna, 116–117
ragout of Jerusalem artichokes à la Provençale, 196
veal, from the South, 163
white bean, 244
winter beef daube from Die, 149–150
strawberry:
compote, 279
tart, 259
stuffed saddle of lamb, roasted, 177
sugar syrup for fruit sauce, 284
summer delight, 283
summer pudding, blueberry and raspberry, 274–275
sweetbreads with rosemary and preserved lemons, 167
syrup, sugar, 284

tapenade, 19
tarragon:
dressing, shrimp in, 106
fresh, consommé with, 69
veal shanks braised with pearl onions and, 164–165
tarte:
aux abricots, 263
campagnarde à l'oignon, 89
campagnarde aux cerises, 262
aux citrons confits, 257–258
au clafoutis de cerises, 261
au clafoutis de framboises, 264
aux clémentines, 254–255
aux figues fraîches, 266
aux fraises, 259
galette aux pommes, 268
à la mozzarelle fumée, 91
aux myrtilles, 265
aux noix, 270
aux poires et aux amandes, 269
nyonsaise, 90
princesse à la confiture d'abricots, 256
renversée aux prunes, 267
à la rhubarbe, 260
St. Tropez, 271–273
au soufflé de tomates et basilic, 92–93
tarts, 250–251
almond and apricot jam, 256
apple galette, 268

apricot, 263
blueberry, 265
candied lemon, 257–258
caramelized upside-down plum, 267
cherry clafoutis in, 261
clementine, 254–255
country cherry, 262
country onion, 89
fresh fig, 266
nut, 270
pear and almond, 269
prebaked shells for, 253
raspberry clafoutis in, 264
rhubarb, 260
smoked mozzarella, 91
strawberry, 259
tomato, cheese, and olive, 90
tomato and basil soufflé in, 92–93
tendrons de veau, 160
grillés, 162
poêle à la dioise, 160–161
terrines:
de jambon aux courgettes, 25
ham and zucchini, 25
ratatouille, 225–226
tétragone à l'ail, 231
thon, daube de, à la provençale, 116–117
tians:
d'agneau aux aubergines, 179–180
d'aubergines du comtat venaissin, 200
d'aubergines et de poivrons rouges au fromage, 201–202
d'aubergines et de tomates Vieux Télégraphe, 20
de tomates, 233
see also gratins
toasts, 79
tomates:
coulis de, avec les tomates en boîte, 10
coulis d'été de, 8–9
farcies à l'agneau, 172–173
farcies à la tomme et au basilic, 22–23
fraîches, soupe aux, 65
lapin à la sarriette et au coulis de, 137
pâtes fraîches à la marmelade de poivrons et aux, 87
petits soufflés de, 93
pissaladière aux poivrons rouges et aux, 86
à la Provençale, 232
provençales légères, 232
salade de poivrons et de, 48
tarte au soufflé de basilic et, 92–93
tian d'aubergines et de, Vieux Télégraphe, 20
tian de, 233